Best Wi

Dennis Ludwig.

MW01254089

Advice to my Son

30 Year Anniversary Limited Edition

[redacted]

Dennis M. Ludwig

FriesenPress

One Printers Way
Altona, MB R0G 0B0
Canada

www.friesenpress.com

Copyright © 2022 by Dennis M. Ludwig
First Edition — 2022

All rights reserved.

No part of this publication may be reproduced in any form, or by any means, electronic or mechanical, including photocopying, recording, or any information browsing, storage, or retrieval system, without permission in writing from FriesenPress.

Original written by D.M. Ludwig in February 1991. Revised in 2021.

[redacted]

ISBN
978-1-03-913438-6 (Hardcover)
978-1-03-913437-9 (Paperback)
978-1-03-913439-3 (eBook)

1. FAMILY & RELATIONSHIPS, PARENTING, PARENT & ADULT CHILD

Distributed to the trade by The Ingram Book Company

Table of Contents

Note from the Author

DUE TO MARITAL DIFFICULTIES, our family split up with my son staying with his mother and my daughter living with me, her father. This book was written for my son because I wasn't there to give him advice during all the everyday situations he faced. I don't view things much differently today than when I wrote the book thirty years ago. As you get older, you tend to think about the predominant thoughts of your youth.

Why did I decide to share this book with the world? I did it in the hope that readers will use some of my ideas to make the world a better place.

Foreword

Written by my daughter, Lanette

MY DAD WAS FORTY-SIX years old when he immersed himself in the writing of this book, his passion project. His mission: to transcribe everything he had learned in his lifetime into a playbook for my younger brother, who lived with my mother apart from us. I distinctly remember because I was the one who typed and formatted the document based on my dad's handwritten pencil scratches, before word processors were widely available. We photocopied and hole-punched the pages before inserting them into clunky plastic binders. Even though this manual of life was not written for me, my dad gifted me a copy as payment for my efforts, which then sat in a storage box for decades, collecting dust.

That was thirty years ago. My father is now nearing eighty years old. He still tells the same stories with an ever-present twinkle in his eye. But his physical health is deteriorating and his frequent ambulance rides to the hospital remind me of how precious life is. Because of the pandemic, it was not possible to be by his side to support him in person. Consumed with worry, yet helpless to do anything, I reflect back to the young, single dad who raised me—a troubled adolescent daughter—on his own. Memories of the two of us together, trying simultaneously to figure out the world and each other, brings me tears, laughter and gratitude.

He was in the hospital emergency room and on my mind when I experienced a near fatal car accident on a single-lane highway. As I crawled out of the wreckage of my crumpled car, I was shaken and in a state of shock. In the days that followed, my body slowly recovered, but my mind couldn't stop reliving the moment of impact and questioning the meaning of my life. How was I still here and what was I meant to do?

The answer lay in an old, dusty storage box, in the manual of life that I had not seen for three decades. I felt pulled toward the comforting words of my father.

Dennis Murray Ludwig was born on November 12, 1945. Along with being the first of the Baby Boomer generation, he was also the first of nine children who were born and raised on a tiny farm in the heart of the Canadian prairies.

Based on the tales told, life on the farm was simple, but never easy. Survival was dependent on the forces of nature, the good will of neighbours and a strong faith in God. With eleven people in my grandparents' house, sacrifices often had to be made to ensure there was enough to go around. Humility and hard work were considered virtues. Life lessons were learned while harvesting the land, tending to the flock and swimming in the dugout. I grew up hearing about the mischief my dad and his friends would get into and the practical jokes they would play. Love and laughter was intertwined into every story.

When my dad graduated from high school in 1962, his mother sat him down and told him he had to find his way in the big city. There was no room for him to come back to live on the farm. My dad didn't take offense to this. He understood this was the reality of the situation. So off he went, a seventeen-year-old, naive farm boy, to forge his path.

He started college, poor and hungry, with a talent for numbers. Early on, he established an underground poker ring for students and then received a stern warning from academic administrators to cease and desist. He ultimately graduated, secured a job, bought his first car—a 1967 Mustang—married my mother and had two children—myself and my brother—before his mid-twenties. He told us that the most important two days in his life were when my brother and I were born. Growing up, I remember how much fun he was, always making time to play.

When he trained for a marathon, I pedaled my bicycle alongside him for months down dirt roads and into the prairie sunsets. He modelled perseverance in his quest to achieve his goals. He encouraged me to always take the road less travelled, speak truth to power and accept what makes me unique.

When my parents divorced, I cried more tears than I knew were possible. I remember feeling the void when my dad walked away with little more than the shirt on his back. He left my mom everything so that she could provide us with shelter, transportation and other necessities of life. He diligently visited us every second weekend as the custody agreement allowed and every summer we would travel to my grandparents' home to experience life on the farm.

I was twelve years old when I went to live with my dad, despite him being adamantly opposed to raising me. He believed a father was incapable of teaching female life skills—such as cooking, cleaning and sewing—to a daughter. We eventually found common ground, but for years my dad would tell any random person who would listen that he had no business raising a daughter and that he was much better suited to raise a son so he could teach him about sports and girls and cars.

Thirty years ago, my dad wrote this book for my younger brother on his eighteenth birthday. Given that my brother was raised in my mother's care, this book was my dad's attempt at imparting fatherly advice and expressing his love. The document was written with the goal of ensuring my brother was adequately prepared for the life ahead of him and with the hope that he could avoid some mistakes along the way. I remember this because, before writing the words for my brother, my dad practiced his philosophy on me.

My dad isn't perfect. His opinions are not always based on fact. He is humble and stubborn, old fashioned and eccentric. But he is my dad and he has spent his entire life doing the best he could to make a positive impact in this world. This book was my dad's gift to my brother, but it has the potential to be a gift to us all. It's a generational story of one man's love for his child and represents a life well lived. In my search for meaning and purpose, I found his message soothingly simple: Be a good person, make the world a better place and have some fun along the way.

Advice to My Son

HAPPY EIGHTEENTH BIRTHDAY MY son. And congratulations on reaching adulthood. I was a little short on cash this year, so for your birthday present I'm giving you this homemade book. It contains all the important ideas I've picked up over the years. By learning these things at an early age, I hope you won't have to scratch your head quite as often as I did, wondering what the world is all about and what to do about it.

Due to marital disagreements, I left when you were six years old. Since I wasn't there as a role model and teacher during your everyday experiences, I hope this philosophy lesson can replace twelve years of fatherly advice.

I have included many quotations from wise men. These quotations express my ideas better than I can, plus they give credibility to my theories. I've covered quite a few topics for you to think about. Wherever you go, it should be fun. Life is an adventure, not a burden. I've enjoyed writing this, and I hope you enjoy reading it.

* * *

The ideas I stand for are not mine. I borrowed them from Socrates. I swiped them from Chesterfield. I stole them from Jesus, and I put them in a book. If you don't like their rules, whose would you use?

— Dale Carnegie

The Purpose of Life

THE MOST IMPORTANT QUESTION, and one that should affect most of our decisions in life, is: Why are we here?

I look at life as a game. First, everyone is given a brain and a body. The arena where the game is played is called Earth. The object of the game is to get as many brownie points as you can in a lifetime. You get these brownie points by doing good deeds, but you can also lose brownie points with bad deeds. It's an interesting game. If you're good at it, it can be a lot of fun. But as you know from playing soccer, games sometimes demand endurance, suffering and perseverance. And, of course, the longer you stay in the game, the more points you're going to get. So it's a good idea to look after your health and drive safely so you can live a long productive life.

The good news is that, sooner or later, almost everybody wins the game. If you don't get enough brownie points in this lifetime, you can come back and try again and again until you do. After you've mastered this game you get to go to other places and play different games. When you become an expert at all of them you move into the big mansion in the sky called Heaven.

We are here for testing and advancement. We are part of nature and just like the ants are here to make a better anthill and the bees are here to make a better beehive, we are here to make Earth a better place to live. It's not a complicated assignment. If the bees can do it, we should be able to. It just means helping each other, protecting our homes, having babies

…owing them how to live for the good of man and nature. And just …the bees enjoy buzzing around looking for honey, we should enjoy the …me of life. The following pages contain tips on how to have fun while earning brownie points.

* * *

The life not dedicated to the service of mankind is a life wasted.

— Albert Einstein

For when the One Great Scorer comes
To write against your name
He marks not that you won or lost
But how you played the game

— Grantland Rice

Decisions

MAKING DECISIONS IS FUN. I think that's why kids like video games. Making decisions is fun and making correct decisions is even more fun. Let's first look at how decisions are made.

Approximately three percent of our decisions are based on reason. They are made in our conscious mind. The conscious part of the brain gives us what we call our free will. It sets the rules. Do we want to be good or bad? Do we want to get married today? Do we want to buy an ice-cream cone?

The remaining decisions are made in the unconscious mind. They come to us by impulse and intuition. The unconscious mind is like a computer. It can think fast and has a great memory. It remembers everything that has happened to you in this life and can also access information from your soul about previous lives. It is full of fears and hates and loves and talents learned from previous experiences. It is just waiting for your free will to send over a request. Then the unconscious mind does the best job it can for you, within the guidelines that your free will has laid out. This may be best explained by an example.

When you're playing soccer, you may want to get the ball away from an opponent. Your free will sends an order to the unconscious mind saying, "let's get the ball." The unconscious mind says, "Fine, I like a challenge. Now, how should we do this? We could grab him by the hair and punch him in the nose like we used to do on the pirate ship. But we don't want to break the silly soccer rules, so we'll have to do something else. I guess the best way would be to run fast using that little extra push off with the big toe that I learned in ancient Greece. Then I'll kick the ball back to Steve like the coach told me to. Alright. I've got it figured out. Adrenalin, head for the calf muscles. Left leg forward… HERE WE GO."

There are a few tips that help in decision making.

"Follow That Impulse" is a good rule of thumb when you get a brainwave about something trivial. I wouldn't quit my job because I got a flash of brilliance in the mind for an instant but I would follow an impulse when betting on a football game or deciding what colour shirt to wear in the morning.

The governing factor in most decisions is: What is best for mankind? This sometimes requires that we sacrifice our own interests for the good of the majority or for someone in greater need.

Some people are so afraid of making mistakes that they refuse to make decisions. This really confuses the unconscious. These people usually end up going to a psychiatrist for depression and stress problems. They'd be fine if they only realized we're here to learn and mistakes are the best teacher.

Other people get out of making decisions by putting their lives in the hands of the Lord. This reminds me of the story by Michael Hartzell of the man who stayed in his house during a flood:

> First a boat came by and the person in it offered to take him to safety, but he said, "No, the Lord will look after me." The water kept rising, and soon he had to climb up on the roof. A helicopter came over, but the man waved it away saying, "The Lord will protect me." When the water was up to his chest, a log floated near him, but he pushed that away too. Finally, when the water was up to his neck and rising he cried out, "Lord, why didn't you save me?" A booming voice rang out, "I sent you a boat and a helicopter and a log. What more do you want from me?" The man learned, a little late, that the Lord helps those who help themselves.

The risk/reward ratio is another factor that should be considered in our decisions. My favourite example of risk/reward is the following true story:

The tale is told of Dave Randall, who was once the Customer Relations Expert for Scribner's Rare Book Department. Randall had tried relentlessly to obtain one of an old collector's thirteen copies of Thomas Jefferson's Declaration of Independence. The owner stubbornly refused to let go of a single copy. He refused every overture attempted by Dave.

One Friday this owner called Dave Randall and said he had changed his mind. He was now ready to sell. It seemed to just come out of the blue.

Mrs. Randall drove her husband the very next day to meet with the owner. They met at his home in Greenwich, Connecticut. Mr. Randall presented the owner with a cheque and hoped to take possession of the document. The owner balked. Here is a record of the conversation:

"That cheque is not certified," the old seller said rudely.

"But it is not mine; it is Mr. Scribner's personal cheque," complained Randall.

"Can't help that. And what were you intending to do with my property until Monday?" inquired the seller.

"I was going to take it back to my house," replied Randall.

"Might easily burn down."

"Well, it hasn't for one hundred and fifty years," said Mr. Randall, who was getting rather impatient by this time.

"Young man, that won't stop it from burning down tomorrow. I will bring the document in by train on Monday—insured all the way—and bring it to your office, and you will hand me a certified cheque."

"Persnickety old fool," said Mr. Randall to his wife as they drove away.

> On Monday, one of the wisest men in America handed over the document and took the cheque. He had just been told that on Sunday, Mr. Randall's house burned to the ground!
>
> — Steven W. Allen

Life and death decisions are the most interesting. A good example of this can be found in the movie *Lifeboat*. This is also based on a true story.

> A ship sank in the Atlantic and the lifeboat was overloaded. Martin was the highest-ranking crew member on the lifeboat, so he was in command. The water was almost overtopping the lifeboat and he could see a storm coming. He had to decide whether to throw some people over to the sharks or leave everyone in the boat in which case they would probably all die. He decided to get rid of half the passengers. Then he had to decide who to throw overboard.
>
> He finally lightened the boat, and they barely made it through the storm. The next day, they got picked up. The families of the people thrown overboard weren't too happy. They took Martin to court, charging him with murder. All the survivors agreed they wouldn't be alive if Martin hadn't made the bold decision to reduce the load. But he was still found guilty of murder and sentenced to seven years in prison.
>
> — John Steinbeck

I think he should have been given a medal for saving half the passengers. This was a textbook example of how a life-and-death situation should be handled. Do whatever is necessary to save as many as possible.

A lot of times you can tell what to do by using the health-o-meter test (deciding what's best for your health). For example, resentment and hatred hurt us more than the person we direct them against, so the health-o-meter tells us not to hate. Sometimes, it gets a little more complicated. Sex is normally good for the health, but not if it's with another man's wife and if he comes home, he's closer to the butcher knife than you are. Never underestimate the importance of the health-o-meter test.

Driving a car is the next order of business. Since you are already a better driver than me, I can only give you advice on how not to drive.

When parallel parking, most people turn back too late. When meeting another car at night, look to the right side of the road. When backing up, don't go any further than necessary.

In the interests of simplifying decisions before a crisis, you should have a priority list in case of a traffic emergency. My priority list is as follows:

1. Never hit a child. Better to smash into parked cars or hit a pole. I would rather die trying to save the life of a child than feel guilty about their death for the rest of my life.
2. If an animal runs in front of your car, don't endanger yourself to avoid hitting it, only swerve. Don't stop unless you are certain it is safe to do so. Better a dead animal than a dead person.

Another decision-making tool is simplification by exaggeration: an example is whether or not to throw garbage out of the car. Ask yourself, "What if everybody did this?" The answer makes it obvious that it's the wrong thing to do.

And last, but my favourite tiebreaker, is when you've used all the facts and logic but still can't decide between two alternatives: choose the boldest. It will usually be the best.

Once you have made a decision, it's time to implement it. Don't worry about the outcome. You'll win some and lose some. The worst that can happen is you die, in which case all your troubles are over. So do all your worrying and thinking before you make the decision. Then proceed confidently, relax and enjoy watching the outcome.

* * *

Nothing will ever be attempted if all possible objections must first be overcome.

— Jules W. Lederer

The most important questions in life are really only problems of probability.

— Pierre Simon De Laplace

First impulses are nearly always good.

— Charles Talleyrand

Do not do unto others what you do not want done unto yourself.

— Confucius

In matters of principle, stand like a rock. In matters of taste, swim with the current.

— Thomas Jefferson

I am a citizen, not of Athens or Greece, but of the world.

— Socrates

Life is like a game of cards. The hand that is dealt you represents fate; the way you play it is free will.

— Jawaharlal Nehru

I am the master of my fate, I am the captain of my soul.

— William Ernest Henley

Problems

PROBLEM-SOLVING IS MORE DIFFICULT than decision-making. Decisions merely require the selection of an answer. Problem-solving requires the calculation or creation of an answer. For creative ideas, it is best to use the unconscious mind.

Problem-solving is an art. First, you must identify the problem. Gather all the information you can on the subject. Consider all the reasonable courses of action. At bedtime go over the problems and hope for, even expect, a solution to be waiting for you in the morning. Then relax. Sleep on it. Let the unconscious mind work without all the interference it gets during the day from your free will.

Each evening, Thomas Edison would think about the things he hoped to accomplish the next day. Sometimes he would make a list of the jobs he wanted to do and the problems he hoped to solve. Edison also used to take catnaps during the day. When stumped by something, he would stretch out in his workshop and, half dozing, get an idea from his unconscious mind to help him around his difficulty.

Uncle Ronnie keeps a notebook by his bedside to jot down creative ideas as soon as he wakes up.

Sir Walter Scott is reported to have said to himself whenever his ideas wouldn't jell, "*Never mind, I shall have it at seven o'clock tomorrow morning.*"

I find that if you're expecting an answer from the unconscious, you should lie in bed for half an hour after you wake up. This enables the answer to get to your conscious mind without too much interference. If you jump up as soon as the alarm rings, your brain may be so busy thinking about bathroom duties that it won't see the answer the unconscious has flashed down.

Imagine that you have asked a person to phone you in the morning to tell you how the Jets did. The next morning, you crank the stereo up so high you don't hear the phone ring. That would be very rude and after a few times like that I don't think you'd be getting too many morning phone calls. Similarly, the unconscious mind is not stupid. If you don't listen to the answers it provides, it will soon learn to save the effort of figuring out your problems.

* * *

The best thinking has been done in solitude; the worst has been done in turmoil.

— Thomas Edison

Happiness

HAPPINESS SEEMS TO BE a desirable goal because happy people tend to be healthier, perform better and think better.

But what is happiness? It's the pleasant thoughts that come with striving for a goal. This goal could be anything from playing for a soccer championship, learning how to drive a car, creating an affectionate relationship with your girlfriend, raising children or helping a blind person cross the street. You should have no difficulty finding happiness because there are lots of goals you can strive for.

Everybody wants to be happy. In fact, everything people do is motivated by the desire to be happy. Yet most people are unhappy. Why? Two reasons: They either have no goals, or they have stopped striving for goals.

Many Hollywood stars are constantly having fun by going to parties, buying fancy new cars and living life in the fast lane. Yet, in memoir after memoir, these celebrities reveal that hidden under all their fun is a life of depression, alcoholism, drug addiction, broken marriages, troubled children and profound loneliness.

Why are these people unhappy? Because they don't have any goals to strive for. They could become happy by helping other people, but these celebrities are too selfish to spend their time and money doing good deeds. I guess they aren't aware that one of the most pleasant thoughts a person can have is the thought that they are needed, that they are important to the happiness of another human being.

The moment we understand that material things don't bring happiness we begin to lead our lives differently. We no longer have to chase the glamorous life of the rich and famous. We have more time for doing things that really increase our happiness. We even save money because it's no longer so important to buy those new clothes or fancy cars.

What about the non-celebrities that we see around us every day? They should have enough goals, so why are they so unhappy? It's because they don't strive to reach their goals. Instead, they feel sorry for themselves and resent the people around them. They should learn, and if we get an opportunity we should teach them that no one can decide what your thoughts will be but yourself.

There are always facts in the world and in our personal lives that justify either a pessimistic outlook or a happy one. It's just a matter of what we choose to think about. Your mom used to say that if I was in a barrel of shit up to my neck, I would be happy that it wasn't up to my mouth. She was right.

If you can't think of a way to achieve your goals, you've got a problem. But even then, you might as well be happy because you're more likely to think of a solution if you're in a good mood. Some of the happiest times in my life were when I was practicing for the marathon or studying for a chess tournament. These were not particularly enjoyable activities but I had a goal and when a man is striving for a goal, he tends to feel happy regardless of the circumstances.

In summation, if you want to be happy, keep yourself well supplied with goals. If you want to be extra happy, help someone else strive for a goal.

* * *

Play will be my next topic. Play regularly! I don't know why I am even mentioning this topic to you because you've never indicated any reluctance to play but here I go anyway.

Jesus said we must become like little children before we can enter the kingdom of heaven. There is nothing more characteristic of little children than their love of play. No one comes into this world a workaholic. Children don't care about work or money or power or what we call achievement.

It's only after we have been criticized by intellectuals, economists and psychologists that we change our view of the universe.

In many societies, such as the Greek and Roman societies, people enjoyed themselves. Nowadays, the bright boys from university have turned life into a war zone where we are in a constant battle for material possessions. If we refuse to play their silly game, we are called failures.

This reminds me of the American foreign aid worker in India. He saw some farmers sitting around playing cards, so he asked one farmer why he wasn't out working in his field:

The farmer said, "Why should I do that?"

The young advisor, happy to show off what he had learned in university, replied, "So you can grow more grain. Then you will make more money and be able to buy a tractor and farm more efficiently. Eventually, you'll be rich enough to buy more land and hire workers to do all the work."

"Why should I do that?" the farmer still wanted to know.

"So you can sit around and play cards!" the expert replied.

Health considerations are another reason to play. Studies have shown that hard physical work does not reduce the risk of heart attack. Yet, physical activity in leisure time does reduce the chance of disease. Swimming, running, gardening and tennis are much more useful than hard work when it comes to building good health.

Appearances are not the most important thing in life. However, in order to attract people you are interested in you must also be attractive to them. This is why we do such things as lose weight or buy a new shirt. Similarly, if it makes you feel more confident, I see nothing wrong with wearing an earring, dying your hair or having plastic surgery. These changes are done not to deceive people, but to make our physical appearance match our desired self-image. If there is nothing wrong with changing our mental attitude in order to gain happiness, I see nothing wrong with changing our physical appearance for the same reason.

* * *

What one sees depends on what one is looking for.

— John Lubbock

Life must be lived as play, playing certain games, singing and dancing.
— Plato

Career

A CAREER IS AN excellent opportunity for self-development. Each of us brings his own unique combination of talents into this life. One may have an aptitude for mathematics, someone else may have a great sense of humour and another person may be good at riding horses. How we use these talents is up to us. The ability to coach a soccer team or cook a tasty, healthy meal gains just as many brownie points as designing a spaceship.

You may decide to choose a career that uses your unconscious talents or you may decide on one that gives you the opportunity to develop entirely new talents. It's up to you. As long as you're associating with people, you will have opportunities to develop your skills and virtues for the benefit of mankind.

You don't have to waste your life in a job that doesn't excite you. There are so many other things you could do if you only took the time to look into them. Daydream! What did you always want to be when you grew up? What do you dream of today? Is there any reason you shouldn't at least try to make your life what you want it to be? Did you want to be a lion tamer? Maybe you can be one. If not, you might be able to find another interesting job dealing with animals.

You don't have to reject your own interests and live by someone else's code. You don't have to follow the ideas that the majority has decided are right. History is full of examples where people who dared to be different were ridiculed by the masses.

In 1903, Orville and Wilbur Wright invented and flew the first airplane. Most newspaper editors discounted the witness reports and dismissed the story without even printing this momentous news. For many years, the brothers tried to find a market for their new flying machine. In a letter to the inventors in 1907, the First Lord of the Admiralty wrote, "The Board of Admiralty were of the opinion that airplanes would not be of any practical use to the Naval Service."

In 1610, when Galileo's telescope revealed Jupiter's moons, his fellow astronomers refused to look through it. They knew that such bodies were not possible, therefore the telescope must be deceptive. So, why look through it?

In 1878, Thomas Edison demonstrated his new electric light bulb at the World's Fair in Paris. Professor Erasmus Wilson wrote, "With regard to the electric light, much has been said for and against it, but I think I may say without fear of contradiction that when the Paris exhibition closes, electric light will close with it and very little more will be heard of it."

Dr. Semmelwies developed the theory of bacteria in 1860 and his ideas saved hundreds of lives. Yet scientists scorned his theory and drove him out of Vienna and out of his mind. The value of his work was not recognized until twenty-five years later, after his death.

So don't feel bad if people laugh at your ideas. You'll be in good company.

The most important consideration in the selection of a career should be: How can I best be of service to mankind while at the same time doing something that I enjoy? The financial aspects should be of secondary importance. If you are contributing to the welfare of humanity, sooner or later the rewards will come your way.

Your attitude toward your job has a lot to do with how much satisfaction you get from life. A good example of the proper attitude was shown in a story called "A Message to Garcia" by Elbert Hubbard.

> In 1899 the Spanish-American war broke out when the United States supported the Cuban rebels fighting to gain their independence from Spain. U.S. President McKinley wanted to communicate with the leader of the rebels. Garcia was somewhere in the mountains of Cuba—no one knew where. No mail or telegraph could reach him. The president needed to secure his cooperation, and quickly. What to do?

Someone said to the president, "There is a fellow by the name of Rowan who will find Garcia for you, if anyone can."

Rowan was sent for and given a letter to be delivered to Garcia. Rowan took the letter, sealed it up in an oilskin pouch and strapped it over his heart. In four days, he had landed at night off the coast of Cuba in an open boat and disappeared into the jungle. Three weeks later, Rowan came out on the other side of the island, having travelled across a hostile country on foot and delivered his letter to Garcia.

The point is, the president gave Rowan a letter to be delivered to Garcia. Rowan took the letter and did not ask, "Where exactly is he?"

This is how you do a job. Be loyal, act promptly, concentrate your energies and do the thing. Carry a message to Garcia.

Someday you may get into a management position. I am no expert in this area, but I have observed one thing: Good managers practice what they preach. Employees don't have much respect for or loyalty to a boss who says, "Do as I say, not as I do."

My favourite management story involves the owner of a steel mill, Henry J. Kaiser:

One day, Mr. Kaiser was walking in the company yard when he noticed the gravel on the road and walkways was a reddish colour. He asked the foreman about this and was told it was because the rocks were left over from melting the ore in the foundry. Apparently, a small amount of iron must have been left in the rocks, and this was now rusting and causing the red colour.

Kaiser said, "*Load all this rock up and run it through the foundry again.*" The foreman protested that it wasn't economical to melt all that rock for such a small amount of iron. But Kaiser insisted, and he was the boss, so it was done.

From then on, the foundry operator made absolutely sure that every bit of iron was removed from the ore before it was released. Although the company lost money on that batch, it more than made up for it on the thousands of batches that followed.

* * *

He that would be the greatest among you will be the servant of all.

— Jesus Christ

In order for people to be happy in their work, three things are required. They must be fit for it. They must not do too much of it. And they must have a sense of success in it.

— John Ruskin

An hour in the morning is worth two in the evening.

— Chinese Proverb

Genius is 1% inspiration and 99% perspiration.

— Thomas Edison

It is the great triumph of genius to make the common appear novel.

— Goethe

Business

MY FAVOURITE ADVICE ABOUT how to run a business is taken from the book *How I Found Freedom in an Unfree World* by Harry Browne (1973). This information might prove useful for anyone who owns a business.

"The traditional way of structuring business enterprises lead easily to restrictions, bad feelings and conflicts of interests between employers, employees and partners."

The "partnership" isn't a living entity with a single purpose and a single mind. Each of you will remain individuals—with individual motives, talents, goals and attitudes. Your ideas about the business will differ in some ways. For instance, you may each agree to work hard, but work "hard" defies precise definitions. What you each mean by your intentions probably won't be mutually understood until you have a disagreement and one of you thinks the other isn't working hard enough.

Even if you work equally hard, you won't produce the exact same value. The one who's more valuable will be subsidizing the other to some extent. In fact, each of you could come to think that he's the stronger partner and that the other is thereby getting a better deal.

Often, a partnership is established to combine two different talents—one may be the producer and the other the seller. Both functions are essential to the business, but they won't necessarily be equal in value. To share fifty-fifty (or any other ratio) can open the door to resentments.

As in any other type of relationship, if your reward is dependent upon more than your own output, you won't have a 100 percent incentive to produce more. For anything you do, you'll receive only half the reward—the other half going to your partner. As a result, there will be a natural incentive to produce less and to encourage your partner to produce more.

Dozens of other problems are inherent in partnerships. If you've ever been in one, you probably know them all. You may feel that you made a bad choice of partners, but it's more likely you made a bad choice of structures.

Action involves thinking, deciding, valuing and doing—by one human being. Each person should control and evaluate his own action. Unfortunately, the normal ways of operating a business overlook these principles. They amalgamate individuals into groups and hope for collective action.

If a relationship is structured so that each person has his own area of responsibility over which he has complete control, most of the typical headaches of a business can be eliminated. This should be clearer as we apply these principles to a business enterprise.

Suppose you have an idea for a product or service you think would succeed in the market. You won't have the talents or time necessary to do everything in the business, but that doesn't mean you have to take on a partner, nor even that you need employees.

For instance, you're not going to construct your own computer, mill your own stationary or operate your own telephone company. Other people will do those things, but you wouldn't think of taking them into your business as partners—nor would you hire them as employees to be paid on an hourly or weekly basis. You'll contract with them—but only for what you need from them. Why can't you contract for any service you need?

You may not even know how to produce the product you want to market. If that's the case, find someone who can produce it—but don't make him your partner. Find out how much he'll charge you to manufacture the product for you. Then check with other potential manufacturers to determine your alternatives. Pick the one that offers you the most of what you want. You can check the marketplace at any time to see if you're getting the best possible deal from your supplier—but you can't do that with a partner.

You can acquire any service you need in the same way. Perhaps you don't even know how to operate a business. Find someone who does. Then find someone else who does and perhaps even someone else. See what each has to offer and at what price. Select the best one to run the business for you, and pay him on a basis that makes his income an incentive to provide exactly what you want. Define what it is you want from him—and pay him as he provides that.

In the same way, you can contract for every service necessary to make the business work. You don't have to acquire partners or employees. You simply contract with people to provide whatever you need. If you need a salesperson for your product, find one and pay him on the basis of how much he sells. Don't pay him for the time he spends in the office; compensate him on the basis of sales.

When you pay for results, not for time, you get three important benefits: (1) You have an accurate understanding of what each thing costs you (and can easily compare alternatives); (2) you no longer have to supervise the individual's time—all you have to do is check his results; and (3) each supplier has the same incentive you do with regard to his service—he'll profit most by doing what is most valuable to you.

It's important, too, that you don't try to create group incentives. Don't offer to pay someone on the basis of the net profits of the business. He doesn't control the amount of net profit with his one service, so he has little incentive to try to increase it.

The only exception to paying for results might be when hiring a manager to run the business. He would be in a position to affect the profits—so you might decide to pay him based on the net profits of the business.

Very few people are stupid; it's just that most employees have no real incentive to use their intelligence in their jobs. They reserve their mental energy for their hobbies, personal relationships and other things outside the office. In fact, with normal compensation systems, an employee often uses most of his initiative figuring out how to work less without losing his job. With the right system, that mental energy can be unleashed on your behalf.

Another benefit of this system is that it allows you to begin with much less capital—and thus, with less risk. You pay for things only as you need them; there's no weekly payroll that must be met regardless of the need for it. As a result, you need fewer permanent facilities.

Even if you don't have enough money to begin, you don't have to take in a partner. You can pay interest on borrowed money. Arrangements whereby an investor is made a partner is risky. If the business is a success, you'll be sharing your profits long after you need the initial capital. While that's a decision you might willingly make, you may regret it five years later. And taking in a partner always opens the door to joint decisions and disagreements.

There's a whole world of its own involved in business compensation systems. But you can probably work out a very effective one yourself if you keep the three basic principles in mind:

1. *Deal with each individual on an individual basis. Make sure his compensation is dependent only upon his own value to you.*
2. *Contract only for what you want. Determine what results you want from someone, and pay for those results only. If he delivers, you needn't worry about how he uses his time—that's not your concern.*
3. *Don't attempt to perpetuate a relationship by contract. If any contracts are necessary, make them for the shortest practical period of time, with ways of terminating with relatively short notice. Try to avoid any situation in which someone is obligated to perform services beyond the time in which it's in his self-interest to do so. You won't get good value when the individual no longer wants to be involved.*

I've seen a number of businesses operated profitably in this way. The owners of those businesses avoid the normal problems that most businesses take for granted. Employees are more devoted to their work, very little supervision is required, costs are clearly discernable and the lowest cost available is commensurate with quality.

I once had a similar experience. I was operating a small business in California—burdened with payroll taxes, bookkeeping requirements and other regulations imposed by the government. There were social security taxes, unemployment insurance taxes, disability insurances taxes and income taxes to be paid or withheld. They cost me money and time, and they reduced the take-home pay of employees. The business had been losing money so fast it was about to go under. I fired all the employees (including myself).

I asked for bids from the marketplace—inviting employees and outside businesses to submit prices for performing the necessary functions. Their resulting costs were far less than the previous expenses.

The employees who continued to work with me became independent contractors. They performed specific services—in their own way and at their own pace—for which they were paid a specific fee for each service. Rules were set only for the quality of the service and the delivery deadlines.

The "employees" of my company received an additional benefit. They were now independent business people, selling their services to me, so they could designate their homes as their offices instead of coming to my office to perform services for me. As a result, each of them had far more tax deductions. They could claim business deductions for part of their household expenses, telephone bills, utility bills, car expenses and other things that are normally considered to be personal expenses. Even with no income tax withheld, very few of them owed anything in taxes at the end of the year.

None of them bothered to file quarterly tax estimates, and none of them ran into trouble from the Internal Revenue Service.

The simple change from employee status to that of independent contractor resulted in lower taxes for everyone concerned. It's a small and common example—but there are probably millions of people who could use that loophole and don't. Since I no longer had any employees, I no longer paid or withheld payroll taxes. No bureaucrat called me to find out why the revenue to the state had been lost.

The new system changed the business into a profitable venture and made the work more profitable and enjoyable for every individual concerned. Those who continued to work with me made more money per hour worked, and I was able to cut my working time by about half. Nothing else changed but the system of compensation—and that one change provided many benefits.

Even if you don't operate a business, you're in a better position if you act as a supplier of a service rather than as an employee. You can contract with companies to perform specific services for them at specific prices. In addition to the tax benefits, you can choose your own working hours, usually make more money and have more free time.

— Harry Browne

* * *

The shortest and best way to make your fortune is to let people see clearly that it is in their interest to promote yours.

— Jean La Bruyère

If it's a job worth doing it's worth doing well.

— Chesterfield

The best worker is the man who sees what has to be done and does it.

— Edward Adrian Wilson from *Scott's Last Voyage*

The best argument is that which seems merely an explanation.

— Dale Carnegie

It is a sign of a superior man to disagree and yet remain friendly.

— Gene Telpner

If two people agree all the time, one is an idiot. If two people disagree all the time, both are idiots.

— Darryl Zanuck

There is never enough time to do it right the first time, but there is always enough time to do it over again.

— John W. Bergman

Short sentences, dry voice; that is a leader talking.

— Unknown

The executive exists to make sensible exceptions to general rules.

— Elting Morrison

No one has ever been able to purchase such ultimate treasures as a good family, sound health, true friends, loyal employees, true love or true respect.

— Kingsley Ward

A man with a new idea is a fool until the idea succeeds.

— Mark Twain

Friends

EACH OF US IS in a constant battle against boredom. Having friends and enemies helps us fight this boredom. Although enemies supply us with the most interesting thoughts, these thoughts have been found to be harmful to the health of both body and soul. Consequently, I try to ignore my enemies as much as possible and concentrate on my friends.

There is no safe code of conduct that will please everyone. Our actions can always be condemned for one reason or another… too bold for some, too cautious for others. Every fool is entitled to his own opinion.

A few people will dislike you for no reason whatsoever, even after you've done your best to be friends with them. When this happens, all you can do is throw up your hands and remember the adage—you can't cuddle a porcupine.

If you want to find someone with similar interests, you should look where such people are likely to be found. If you like rock music, you probably won't meet someone with the same musical tastes at the opera. As Ann Landers says, "*You can't expect to catch a trout in a sucker barrel.*"

Since you can meet potential friends almost anywhere, it's important to display your real qualities openly and honestly wherever you are. Then others can recognize the real you. Those who disapprove will seek someone different to be with and those who have standards similar to yours will act favourably toward you. You won't have to hide facts and worry about what role you should be playing.

There is no need to feel bad if you can't or choose not to keep up with the latest trends. Popular trends are only part of public opinion. In fact, they are usually not even representative of the majority of the people. They are simply given a lot of publicity.

Friends are people with whom you have one or more important things in common. You really get to know a person when you work together on a project that is important to both of you. You learn to maintain an attitude of hopefulness and helpfulness. You also learn that if your friends have to be perfect, you won't have many friends.

Racism

Historically, race determined who people associated with. In reality, though, racism is simply nonsense. There are more important reasons to dislike a person than the colour of their skin.

Intelligence

I believe people have approximately the same overall intelligence; however, different people are good at different things. This depends on what experiences they've gone through in this and previous lives.

Flattery

Compliments are a good way to increase someone's self-esteem. They should be given in a way that doesn't require the receiver to acknowledge the compliment. The method I find works best is to talk indirectly, as if you are talking to yourself. For example, "Wow, she even looks good without makeup," or "What a gorgeous yellow dress!"

A question is an excellent way to give a compliment. If, instead of telling Ken that you think he has a wonderful garden, you ask him for advice about your own, you accomplish three things. You have indicated that you admire his gardening skills. You have singled him out from the crowd. And he can give you advice without having to acknowledge the compliment.

* * *

A friend is someone who knows your faults and likes you anyway.

— Elbert Hubbard

One friend in a lifetime is much, two are many, three are hardly possible.

— Henry Adams

Great minds discuss ideas, average minds discuss events, small minds discuss people.

— Eleanor Roosevelt

People never get hysterical alone, but just when they have an audience.

— Chuck Palahniuk

When a man says not exactly, he means exactly.

— Unknown

The best way to gain an entrance is to assume one.

— Encyclopedia sales manual

The secret to being a bore is to tell everything.

— Voltaire

Insanity is better than boredom.

— Irene Peter

Fish and guests smell in three days.

— Benjamin Franklin

He who excuses himself, accuses himself.

— Ann Landers

Mistakes are often forgiven, but contempt never is.

— Chesterfield

By nature, men are nearly equal.

— Confucius

Everyone is a prisoner of his own experiences. No one can eliminate prejudices—just recognize them.

— Edward Morrow

Common sense is the collection of prejudices acquired by the age of eighteen.

— Albert Einstein

A wise man makes his own decisions; an ignorant man follows public opinion.

— Chinese proverb

Anything you say, whether you say you were joking or didn't really mean it, that's what you really believe.

— Unknown

Romance

PRIOR TO MARRIAGE, LET OTHERS BE FREE should be the motto of any romantic relationship. This period in your life should be spent preparing for marriage by determining your likes and dislikes. As you know, learning is best done by trial and error, so try different places to live, different jobs, different girls, different sexual positions, different foods. Up until the age of thirty, a person is constantly changing. During this period, relationships should be viewed as learning experiences.

It isn't normal for romance to last indefinitely. Human beings are polygamous by nature. A study of rats showed that after a male rat had intercourse with the same female rat 500 to 600 times, he became impotent if brought into contact with that same female. However, if a new female rat was introduced, the male rat regained his virility and went through the same cycle. Human beings can experience the same sexual and emotional boredom with each other.

When you find a girl you like very much, don't get carried away and try to impose your own tastes on her. You don't have to agree on everything. In fact, I think it would be quite boring to be with someone who thought exactly as I do. Let the relationship evolve as it will. If you let others be free, you'll be a rare and valuable person. You'll be in demand because you won't create the conflicts and arguments that possessive people do. How many times have you heard someone say "He smothers me, I need breathing space"?

Your mom once had a poster that said, "If you love something, set it free. If it comes back, it's yours. If it doesn't, it never was." Your mom and I had some good times together, but today I think we're both happier because we followed the advice on that poster.

* * *

Get laid as often as possible.

— Joseph Kennedy

There is nothing that gives more confidence than a full wallet.

— Unknown

All great lovers have the ability to convince the girl of the moment that she is the only woman in the world for him.

— Unknown

Power is the ultimate aphrodisiac.

— Henry Kissinger

Whether a pretty woman grants or withholds her favours, she always likes to be asked for them.

— Ovid 17 AD

We should be careful to get out of an experience only the wisdom that is in it—and stop there—lest we be like the cat that sits down on a hot stove lid. She will never sit down on a hot stove lid again, and that is well; but also she will never sit down on a cold one anymore.

— Mark Twain

Marriage

WHEN OR IF YOU decide to marry is your decision. This is probably the most important decision you will have to make in your life. The decision essentially boils down to, "Will I ever find anyone better for me?" There is no way to know if you should buy a certain house or wait until next month and a better deal might come along.

Is marriage necessary? Certainly not. But having a family is one way to help yourself by helping others. Raising good children helps develop their souls, and this helps your soul. Two parents are better than one if they provide the child with good role models and an example of a good working relationship between adults.

Marriage can lead to many different paths:

1. Successful marriage—the chances are one in five hundred but it has been done.
2. Marry and divorce—the normal roller coaster ride.
3. Marry and tolerate—continuing to live together after the love and communication have stopped is worse than #2.
4. Marry and cheat—I'd imagine the guilt feelings would raise hell with the digestive system.
5. Open marriage—both partners agree to outside affairs. This is difficult for most people to accept.

It has been estimated that you could live compatibly with one out of every five hundred members of the opposite sex. Fortunately, we can improve the odds a bit by weeding out the undesirables. Three things should be considered when choosing a wife: her physical, mental and spiritual qualities.

The physical part is quite easy to check out. If you feel a twinge in your pants whenever you're with her, she's got the right physical qualities.

Mental considerations will help you avoid marrying someone who will try to dominate you. This can be determined by looking at the girl's role model, her mother.

A person's spiritual qualities can be judged by their level of selfishness. Observe how the girl treats people when she's got nothing to gain from them.

Satisfy all three of the above criteria and you might have a successful marriage. Overlook even one of them and you are asking for trouble.

The purpose of marriage should be to work together to make the world a better place to live. It doesn't matter if there is a marriage certificate, monogamy, polygamy, open marriage, or even orgies, as long as the partners love each other and agree on the details of behaviour.

Marriage is a fifty-fifty proposition. You don't own your wife. She is your companion. You should work together like a mortar and pestle. When having discussions, glance at the negatives but concentrate on the positives. You are supposed to help each other… to encourage, not discourage. There will be a few disappointments and disagreements now and then, but try not to rant and rave during those times. Instead, attempt to reason things out together. The troubles and sorrows in marriage are to teach us that love does not possess.

The greatest sins in the world today are selfishness and domination of one individual by another. Very few people allow others to live their own lives. We tend to tell others how to live. We try to force them to live our way and see things how we see them. Most wives want to tell their husbands what to do, and most husbands want to tell their wives what they can and cannot do. Remember: No one else answers to God for what you do, and you don't answer to God for what others do. We have a right to tell people our own personal experiences and let them decide for themselves, but we have no right to force them to live a certain way.

If either of you becomes selfish or self-centred and satisfies your own sexual desires regardless of the effect this may have on the other person, the home will soon fall apart. A cheated man is a loser, and a cheater never wins. When the trust is gone, there isn't much left.

The highest achievement possible on Earth is to create a home with an atmosphere where ideas and character can be formed. Prepare your home so it's a joyous place for those who come into it, a place where they like to be. Try to establish an air of helpfulness in your home. It should not be a place where others are afraid to come.

I believe the feelings of the occupants of a home stay in the walls. Some homes—like Uncle Dieter's—are full of love, and you enjoy being there. The walls are full of laughter. Yet I have been in some places that I can't wait to get out of.

When we moved into our first home, we were one happy little family. Our new neighbour mentioned to me that our house was eleven years old and we were the seventh family to live in it. He said five of the couples had gotten divorced, and the sixth was having problems when they moved out. Your mom didn't like the house from the first time she set foot in it but I insisted we buy it for all the logical reasons. I wonder if women can sense the bad vibrations in the walls? I wonder if we'd have stayed together as a family, in another house?

Hopefully you will never have to go through a divorce; however, it may happen since we do not control other people's lives. Marriage contracts should not enslave people into miserable, unhealthy relationships. No loving person should have to suffer the torment of living with someone who is mean and selfish. Divorce is just as logical and useful as the cancellation of any other legal contract. The decision of whether or not to go for a divorce should be based on two things: the obligation to the children and the obligation to each other. Rebounds almost never work.

Following the divorce, the best interests of the children should be considered. Children cannot serve two masters, so neither parent should ever attempt to pit a child against the other parent. Your mom and I did a fairly good job of burying the hatchet after the war. I think this helped you and your sister grow up without feeling deprived because of losing one of your parents.

It's probably best for all concerned if the child decides which parent they will live with (if the child is old enough to realize the consequences of their choice, and the chosen parent agrees). I think that by the age of ten a child can make a better decision about where they should live than any parent or judge.

* * *

When Socrates was asked which was preferable, to take or not to take a wife, he replied, "Whichever a man does, he will repent it."

— Socrates

By all means marry. If you get a good wife, you will be happy. If you get a bad one, you will become a philosopher.

— Socrates

One key to a marriage is the unguarded look on a woman's face when her husband is telling a story.

— Bruce Freedman

It takes two to make a marriage a success, but only one to make it fail.

— Louis Samuel

Trust is like a thin thread. Once you break it, it is almost impossible to put it together again.

— Ayub Khan

A second marriage is the triumph of hope over experience.

— Samuel Johnson

Children

THE DECISION TO HAVE children should be made only after much careful thought. You are usually looking at eighteen or more years of responsibility. And no matter how much you may cherish the child, it will restrict your actions. That's why it's almost always better for pregnant teenagers to give their babies up for adoption.

As far as abortion goes, I am against it because it isn't natural to go into the womb and kill an unborn baby. Whatever difficulties that baby would have faced in life, there is some soul who would have been thrilled to have the opportunity to learn from those experiences. And there are always adults who would love to raise a newborn baby. An abortion, therefore, reduces the development opportunities for three souls.

Having a child when the parents are in their twenties is not much better. They've hardly had time to understand themselves and decide what they want from their lives. Their plans and ideas may change many times before they reach the age of thirty. Every child has their own personality so you are virtually inviting a stranger to live in your home for the next eighteen years. I don't think people in their twenties are prepared for that.

When the parents are in their thirties, they are better able to devote themselves to children. Their lifestyles have been clearly established and are less likely to change. Also, their financial situation is usually more stable. A child born to such parents will likely be treated with more consistency and love than one born to younger parents.

Some thought should be given to choosing a name for the child. Names with three syllables often get shortened. Girls' names should be interesting and uncommon. Boys' names should be short and simple.

The purpose of parenthood is to raise independent children. Love and understanding are important to a child. You'll show your love more by respecting his individuality and appreciating him for who he is than by forcing him to be who you want.

If you want your child to realize that he is the master of his fate, encourage him by letting him deal directly with the world as much as possible. Let him experience the consequence of his actions. Naturally, you must protect him from dangerous life-threatening situations. It wouldn't be very useful for him to learn by experience that driving his new bike down Portage Avenue at rush hour could get a boy killed. But, generally, it's good to make mistakes.

Uncle Dieter once said, "There are two ways to teach a child to drink: with two hands on the glass or one. My child will use one!" I think that is an excellent philosophy, if you can afford lots of milk.

If you recognize your child as an individual who is allowed to learn for himself, a genuine friendship can develop between you. He'll be willing to talk to you about his ideas, plans and problems. He won't have to fear the guilt trip that most parents inflict when they disagree with their children's ideas and actions.

Be available to your child. Share your opinions without implying that they are the only correct opinions out there. Let him think of you as a wiser, more experienced person, but not a moral authority who is stopping him from living his own life.

This is especially important at the age of fifteen. At fourteen, children think their parents know everything. At sixteen, they think they know everything (must have something to do with being old enough for a driver's license). But at the age of fifteen, they aren't sure if anybody knows anything. I would advise you to give up all your hobbies while your child is fifteen years old. Sit around waiting to argue and debate whenever they want to (which works out to about twice a week). Be a source of information and opinion about the consequences of various acts.

Teaching children this game of life requires a bit of ingenuity. Encouragement works better than correcting. Correct a child once. If they continue to make the same mistake, let them pay for their mistake by going without something they like. This works better than physical punishment.

There seems to be a natural tendency for parents to focus on what the child is doing wrong and say "don't." For some unknown reason, you get far better results by focusing on the desired result and using the word "do," as in, "Shall we do this?" Show appreciation when the child does something constructive and they will want to do more useful things.

There is very little difference between constructive and destructive criticism. Constructive criticism is preceded by a positive remark. For example, when I was teaching you and your sister math, I found that if I said, "You forgot to change the sign," you both went into a defensive shell and didn't absorb the advice. It becomes destructive because your main thoughts were "I'm not good at math," or "I'm stupid." However, when I said, "You're doing good in this chapter, just remember to change the sign," my prize pupils smiled and remembered the advice. Constructive criticism doesn't sound like criticism.

Education

Mere accumulation of information without sound philosophy is not a complete education. The father who teaches his son that what matters in life is helping others gives him a far better inheritance than wealth or a financial interest in the family business.

The Japanese say: "To teach is to learn." I think I learned more about life from my children than they learned from me. If you decide to become a teacher, you'll really learn a lot about life from your pupils.

* * *

There is only one good, knowledge, and one evil, ignorance.

— Socrates

Success breeds success.

— Mia Hamm

The morals of the nation are made on the soccer pitch.

— Winston Churchill

Doing your best is more important than being the best.

— Cathy Rigby

If you can give your son only one gift, let that gift be enthusiasm.

— Bruce Barton

There will never be a shortage of excuses at your disposal. Excuses are for losers. Winners seek solutions.

— Ray Hudson

It doesn't matter who's right, but what's right.

— Maxwell Maltz

Don't handicap your children by making their lives easy.

— Robert A. Heinlein

The best education is the observation of life.

— Socrates

Imagination is more important than knowledge.

— Albert Einstein

When I was a boy of fourteen, my father was so ignorant I could hardly stand to have the old man around. But when I got to be twenty-one, I was astonished at how much he had learned in seven years.

— Mark Twain

Religion

RELIGION IS A BELIEF in God and how to live your life according to God's will.

Is there a God? There is no concrete evidence that God exists. No one has ever seen Him or taken a picture of Him. No one has ever heard him speak or recorded His voice. However, there is evidence of spiritual things like souls, reincarnation and guardian angels. People have seen souls rise from a body immediately after death, reincarnation is mentioned by reputable psychics like Edgar Cayce and I have had some amazing coincidences that can only be explained by the assistance of a guardian angel. It is doubtful such a complex system could be created without a superior being. Therefore, based on the above indirect evidence, I assume there is some superior being involved in our existence who we can call God.

Each religion promotes the beliefs of a philosopher so people have some guidelines on how to live their lives. This results in wildly varied lifestyles because each philosopher has different beliefs based on their individual experiences growing up. Some religions try to control every detail of a person's life while other religions just give general guidelines on how to live. Since there is no way to know which religion is best, I prefer the less restrictive guidelines which may be just as beneficial on our journey to Heaven. The fewer the rules, the more fun we can have. For this reason, I have chosen to follow the teachings of Buddhism.

The current leader of Buddhism is the Dalai Lama. He says you don't need a religion or have to go to church. You just need compassion and love in all its forms. This is a clear and simple philosophy that allows you the freedom to follow your own path in life while gaining brownie points on your journey to Heaven.

The correct definition of a person is: You are a soul. You inhabit a body.

Your soul has been around for a few thousand years. Your body and brain are eighteen years old.

The soul is a high-frequency electromagnetic charge. There are many forces around us that are invisible to our eyes. Radio and television waves are passing through the walls and everything else in the room, including our bodies. Yet to our eyes these waves are invisible. The same is true of X-rays, ultraviolet rays, alpha rays, beta rays, gamma rays and cosmic rays. Although our weak little eyes cannot see these various high-frequency waves, they do exist. The soul is just another invisible force.

This force remains intact even after the death of the human body. The old body, worn out like an old coat, is discarded and buried. But the electromagnetic force, the soul, survives and retains the lifetime memories of the deceased. This electrical charge can later be infused into the body of a newborn baby.

Before birth, a soul hovers over and around the pregnant mother, looking at the experiences it is likely to have in that environment and deciding if such experiences would be best for its development. This is a bit like a person looking over the various fitness clubs and diet centres to see which place would do him the most good. Sometimes things don't work out quite as expected. Accidents do happen and people change. But generally, what you see is what you get, whether a person is looking for a fitness club, or a soul is looking for a certain environment.

Doctors say that what a woman thinks about during her pregnancy is passed on to the baby. For example, if the mother goes to the symphony a lot, the baby will be interested in music. The doctors are close to the truth. What actually happens is a soul that is interested in music says, "That's the mother for me." At the time the baby is born, the soul enters its body. This is when a person becomes a living soul.

Souls go where they expect to learn the most. For example, a white person who has discriminated against blacks may choose to come back as a black person in order to learn what it's like to be discriminated against. A soul moves up the ladder each time an opportunity to help others is acted upon. Basically, the game seems to be how long it takes the soul to teach the conscious mind not to be selfish.

The soul, after its body dies, remains floating around earth reviewing the lessons of its past life. If it has improved enough, it goes on to other planets for further development (nonphysical). If not, it returns to earth to learn from the experiences of another human life.

Do animals have souls? According to Edgar Cayce animals do have souls but they are a lower class of soul than the ones that occupy human bodies. The reincarnation of animal souls crosses the lines of different animal species. For example, the soul of a tiger may return to inhabit the body of a dog in its next life.

* * *

Religion is a superstition invented by mankind a hundred thousand years ago.

— Albert Einstein

Without recognizing the ordinances of heaven, it is impossible to be a superior man.

— Confucius

Are you not ashamed of heaping up the greatest amount of money and honour and reputation, and caring so little about wisdom and truth and the greatest improvement of the soul?

— Socrates

Leonardo da Vinci meditated on the soul, comparing it with the wind passing through organ pipes. And he proclaimed: "The immortality of the soul, which could not decompose with the composition of the body."

— Leonardo da Vinci

Discussing the unborn baby, da Vinci wrote, "Desires and fears are common to this and all the other members of the woman's body, hence it is to be inferred that one and the same soul controls both bodies."

— Leonardo da Vinci

Dalai Lama Quotes:

- *Just one small positive thought in the morning can change your whole day.*
- *Give the ones you love wings to fly, roots to come back and reasons to stay.*
- *Do not let the behaviour of others destroy your inner peace.*
- *The planet does not need more successful people. The planet desperately needs more peacemakers, healers, restorers, storytellers and lovers of all kinds.*
- *Every day, think as you wake up: Today I am fortunate to be alive; I have a precious human life; I am not going to waste it. I am going to use all my energies to develop myself, to expand my heart out to others, to achieve enlightenment for the benefit of all beings. I am going to have kind thoughts toward others. I am not going to get angry or think badly about others. I am going to benefit others as much as I can.*
- *Whether one is rich or poor, educated or illiterate, religious or nonbelieving, man or woman, black, white or brown, we are all the same. Physically, emotionally and mentally, we are all equal. We all share basic needs for food, shelter, safety and love. We all aspire to happiness and we all shun suffering. Each of us has hopes, worries, fears and dreams. Each of us wants the best for our family and loved ones. We all experience pain when we suffer loss and joy when we achieve what we seek. On this fundamental level, religion, ethnicity, culture and language make no difference.*
- *When you talk, you are only repeating something you already know. But if you listen, you may learn something new.*
- *Our prime purpose in this life is to help others. And if you can't help them, at least don't hurt them.*

- *Through difficult experiences, life sometimes becomes more meaningful.*
- *If it can be solved, there's no need to worry, and if it can't be solved, worry is of no use.*
- *We can reject everything else: religion, ideology, all received wisdom. But we cannot escape the necessity of love and compassion. This, then, is my true religion, my simple faith. In this sense, there is no need for temple or church, for mosque or synagogue, no need for complicated philosophy, doctrine or dogma. Our own heart, our own mind, is the temple. The doctrine is compassion. Love for others and respect for their rights and dignity, no matter who or what they are: Ultimately, these are all we need.*
- *Choose to be optimistic; it feels better.*
- *If you want others to be happy, practise compassion. If you want to be happy, practise compassion.*
- *A heart full of love and compassion is the main source of inner strength, willpower, happiness and mental tranquility.*

— Dalai Lama

Reincarnation

REINCARNATION MEANS THE EVOLUTION of man's soul through many successive lifetimes—sometimes as a man, sometimes as a woman, now as a pauper, then as a prince, here belonging to one race, there to another, until finally the soul has reached perfection. The soul is like the actor who takes different roles and wears different costumes on different nights.

Karma is the abacus on which the gains or losses of the soul are scored from life to life. According to the theory of reincarnation, no effort is wasted. We are penalized for evil conduct and rewarded for constructive effort. Edgar Cayce said we have to come back to Earth about thirty times before we learn enough to go on to other places to learn other lessons. When we finally become perfect, we go to Heaven to live with God for the rest of eternity.

I was first attracted to the theory of reincarnation because it provided a logical answer to the question of why some people suffer so terribly for no apparent reason. In all other ways, nature seemed fair. The rabbit at least had a chance, by changing colour or running fast, to escape from the fox. But a black baby, born into slavery, could not escape from the slave owner by changing colour or running away. Similarly, a baby who is born crippled or blind seems destined to suffer throughout their life, without having done anything to deserve it. Reincarnation explains that these restrictions may occur as a result of mistakes we have made in the past.

Birth deformities are usually due to misconduct in a previous life. This is karma for both the parent and the child. The parent may have shown a lack of concern for pain and misery in a past life. This is not a serious enough offence to deserve having to return to Earth as a cripple himself, but having a handicapped child puts him in a position where he can learn to sympathize with people who have physical problems. Indifference to human suffering causes destiny to place it on our doorstep. If after a couple of these kinds of opportunities he still has not learned to be charitable, perhaps coming back deformed will teach him to sympathize with the handicapped.

Not all birth defects are caused by mistakes in previous lives. Accidents do happen. Just as we may have an accident on the way to work, a baby may have an accident on its way into life. But usually the condition of the baby in the womb is the condition of the baby on the delivery table. Whether or not a difficulty in life is related to one's karma, it is always an opportunity for spiritual growth.

A lifetime of genuine sacrifice for others, such as that shown by Lotta Hichmanova or Albert Schweitzer, might equal five or six sterile existences where progress was slow and the soul fell behind in the parade.

* * *

You must be born again before you can enter the kingdom of heaven.

— Jesus Christ

So you sow, so shall you reap.

— Jesus Christ

Reincarnation is not a half-baked myth; it is a cold, hard fact.

— Edgar Cayce

It is not more surprising to be born twice than once; everything in nature is resurrection.

— Voltaire

None but very hasty thinkers will reject reincarnation on the grounds of inherent absurdity.

— T.H. Huxley

Were an Asiatic to ask me my definition of Europe, I should be forced to answer him: It is that part of the world which is haunted by the incredible delusion that man was created out of nothing, and that his present birth is his first entrance into life.

— Schopenhauer

The body of Benjamin Franklin,
Printer,
Like the cover of an old book
Its contents are worn out
And stripped of its lettering and gilding
Lies here, food for worms,
But his work shall not be lost,
For it will, as he believed, appear once more,
In a new and more elegant edition.

— Benjamin Franklin's self-written epitaph

All the world's a stage,
And all the men and women merely players;
They have their exits and their entrances;
And one man in his time plays many parts,
His acts being seven ages.

— Shakespeare

Virtues

THERE ARE NO SHORTCUTS to knowledge, wisdom or understanding. As you know, you can't just read a soccer book and say, "Now I've got it figured out. I'm a winner. I'm going to join the national team and win a World Cup." You first have to practise your passing and tackling in real games.

Similarly, you can't just read this book and say, "Now I've got life figured out. I'm going straight to Heaven." You first have to practise kindness, patience and sincerity in real life. You have to help others who are having difficulty going up the road to Heaven. Some are blindly trying to find the way, some are discouraged, and some think they're on the right road but they have taken a wrong turn.

You may wonder: What's the best way to gain brownie points? It doesn't take a great deed or act or speech. It just takes gentleness, patience and a smile for others in our normal day-to-day activities.

* * *

Patience is the greatest virtue of all and the least understood. A patient man isn't hasty or short-tempered. He bears life's pains and troubles calmly and without complaint.

Patience comes with the realization that life is continuous and no effort is lost. Reincarnation tells us that time is unimportant because what is begun in one life is often finished in the next. This means there is no rush to get fame and fortune at all costs before you die. There is no need to get upset over all the pains and provocations that come our way.

Self-perfection is a slow, daily, inch-by-inch process. A journey of a thousand miles begins with one step and that step must be taken from the point where you are now. The situation you find yourself in is exactly what is necessary for your development. Use the little opportunities that come your way every day. Encourage the weak with a kind word here and there. Give strength to those who need it by doing little acts of goodwill. When such opportunities are used, new and better opportunities will come along. Be what you should be where you are, and when you have proven yourself, God will give you better ways.

It's easier to accept life's little annoyances when you realize that every difficulty is both a test and an opportunity for advancement. Difficulties should be looked on as stepping stones, not stumbling blocks.

* * *

Honesty is a deceptive virtue. Most people think they can get more out of life and can get ahead faster by being dishonest. In reality, the reverse is true. The rewards of honesty far outweigh the gains of dishonesty.

The following are a few of the problems that come with being dishonest:

1. You have to be constantly on guard, wasting your time and energy to cover up past acts.
2. You miss out on opportunities to be appreciated by others because you're hiding your real self. The people who would like the real you never get to know who you are.
3. Sooner or later, someone is going to become aware of your dishonesty. Since he knows you've been dishonest in the past, he can't trust you now. You reduce your alternatives when your word can't be trusted without question.

You can only be sure of someone's honesty if they are honest with everyone. If they say they only lie when it's absolutely necessary, how can you be sure which situation they consider absolutely necessary? If they say they never lie to their close friends, how can you be sure you haven't done something to be demoted from their close friends list? If they cheat on a little thing like paying their bus fare, why wouldn't they lie to you for something more important?

I would suggest you avoid dishonest people altogether. You never know where you stand with them or if they are going to take advantage of you. Dishonest friends are not worth the feelings of uncertainty they cause us.

There are only three situations which would cause me to be dishonest:

1. When telling a fairy tale to children.
2. When making an obvious joke.
3. When necessary to save my life or the life of someone important to me.

Lying to protect someone else's feelings usually does more harm than good. For example, if Jason says to you, "Do you think my nose is too big?" you could lie and say, "Of course not, Jason." But Jason probably knows the truth already, so he'll lose respect for you because you lied. Also, you will hurt your credibility with anyone else who happens to be listening. They won't know whether to believe you or not when you say something nice to them.

What is the alternative to lying? Do you have to be brutal and hurt Jason in order to be honest? No. Often the brutal truth is only a partial truth. For example, when Jason asks you if his nose is too big, you could say "It sure is!" Would that be truth? Only part of it. It would be more completely honest to say, "You have a large nose, but it doesn't make any difference to me."

* * *

Helpfulness is a virtue. The greatest gifts are lessons of self-help. Give others learning and wisdom. Help them reach their spiritual goals, even if they never realize what those goals are. Teaching children, helping the sick or depressed, assisting people with troubles to get their lives together—these are useful acts of helpfulness.

We now come to indirect ways to help the world. Stay away from them like the plague. You will naturally see other people making mistakes, passing the wrong laws, misinterpreting things. You will see poverty, unfairness and repression. It's easy to feel that society needs an overhaul.

What can you do about it? You could try writing letters to editors and politicians, join movements, try to get the right people elected, march in protest, etc. These are all indirect alternatives. Their success depends on if other people see the light. You could spend the rest of your life trying to educate others but you probably wouldn't change the outcome of any social issue.

When I was your age, there were problems of pollution, overpopulation, drugs, organized crime, law and order, extinction of animal species, government debt, high taxes and disarmament. I must have witnessed at least a hundred different marches and protests concerning these issues. I'm still waiting for the first of these problems to be solved. The world seems to continue on its path, wherever it is going.

Before you join a crusade to deal with a social issue, ask yourself—how much do you really know about the issue? Are you sure the solution you desire won't cause even greater problems? Years ago, for example, the government pressured farmers into using pesticides to improve crop yields. Now they've decided those pesticides are harmful to people and pollute the groundwater. Today the government bans the same pesticides they once promoted.

You may consider entering politics to help the world. Forget it. The world is run by a few multinational corporations. They control the newspapers, televisions and politicians. President John F. Kennedy tried to change the world. He got assassinated. Then his brother tried. He got shot too. The third brother decided not to run for president. He decided he could live with the world the way it is. A wise man.

Confucius died thinking himself a failure. They poisoned Socrates. If these men couldn't change the world in their lifetimes, the chances of us succeeding are mighty slim.

So we can't change the world. It's still an exciting and wonderful place. Just remember the serenity prayer: God grant me the serenity to accept the things I cannot change, courage to change the things I can and wisdom to know the difference.

* * *

Courage often seems to be blind thoughtless bravery but it's not. People who act courageously have specific consequences in mind. They know the results of both acting and not acting. They've decided the consequences of acting are better than the consequences of not acting.

When a cat is cornered and turns to fight with a dog, it has calculated that not to fight is sure death, to fight is only probably death. This courage is not an act of bravery, but an act of desperation.

We don't always know why a person acts courageously, but the person himself knows. It may be expectations of good things to come, fear of being a coward, desire for attention or some other goal.

In order to have courage, you must be convinced you are doing the right thing. Think things out in advance. Consider the various courses of action available and the consequences that could follow each action. Pick out the alternative that seems best. Focus on the benefits that await you and remember them when things get difficult. Then do it. You may be wrong but don't worry about that. If we wait until we are absolutely certain before we act, we will never do anything.

We can develop the courage to handle crisis situations by practising courage in our daily lives. This means acting boldly when faced with the little decisions that come up every day.

* * *

The great end of life is not knowledge but action.

— T.H. Huxley

Patience, in asking for what you want, achieves more than loud noises.

— Unknown

God favours the compassionate.

— Arab proverb

I don't concern myself over things which I have no control.

— Bud Grant

All great men have one thing in common. They are both hated and loved because of their honesty.

— Unknown

Whatever you say, even if you say you meant it as a joke or you didn't mean it, that's what you really believe.

— Unknown

A person's intentions are best disclosed during casual conversations in unguarded moments.

— Unknown

People perceive the truth to be what they already believe.

— Leonardo da Vinci

Fine words and an insinuating appearance are seldom associated with true virtue.

— Confucius

Always do right. This will gratify some people and astonish the rest.

— Mark Twain

Adversity

THE PURPOSE OF ADVERSITY is the alteration of character. We should be thankful for our difficulties if they teach us tolerance, patience and perseverance.

As you go through life, you will meet a few ornery and miserable people. Let all the discourteousness and unkindness come from them. No matter what they say or do, try to treat them as you would like to be treated yourself. You can still stand up for what's right without attacking them vindictively. Defend yourself when necessary, but if you can tolerate a little degrading and humiliation once in a while without fighting back, you'll gain a lot of inner peace. This is true mental superiority. Better that everyone takes advantage of you, than you ever take advantage of anyone else.

There will be times when things go bad. You'll doubt yourself. You'll feel worthless. No one is immune to these negative feelings. God knows how many times I wondered if it was me or the world that was crazy. I'm still not sure. But when I feel this way, I say to myself, "I may not be perfect, I may have faults and weaknesses, I may have gotten offtrack, I may have a long way to go—but I am something and I will make the most of that something." Just keep on being the good person that you are and everything will work out okay.

Keep in mind that perfection is not necessary. Approximations are good enough for all practical purposes.

There will be times when you question the fairness of life. You will see selfish people break the law and disregard the rights of others yet gain more material things than you do. You may say, "What's the use of trying to be good when those bastards get more fun out of life?" It's too bad you can't see the fear, doubt and shame that is in their hearts. They may get more rewards in this life, but they'll pay dearly in their next lives.

So far, you don't seem to be suffering too much. You may be quite advanced in soul development, and you may get a chance in this life to see if you can handle power without becoming corrupt. If you get the chance, use it wisely.

* * *

I don't think we should spend too much time or effort trying to bring about justice in the world unless we have chosen a career in the police force. The bad people will get what they deserve, sooner or later. However, if the Lord lays an opportunity in front of us to help Him bring justice in the world, we shouldn't step around it. Hitting a burglar in the ribs with a baseball bat might be a good object lesson for him.

Society has the right to protect itself against the criminal. Justice is an impersonal application of the laws that society has agreed on; it is not an emotional act of vindictiveness. Lawbreakers are punished for the good of the majority. The punishment is not done for revenge but for its deterrent effect. I believe that society's administration of justice should reflect the laws of karma: An eye for an eye, a tooth for a tooth.

* * *

Getting revenge is a mistake. If an innocent man—after suffering injustice at the hands of a powerful enemy—takes a "just" revenge, then they both must come back to Earth in order to learn not to hurt people. If, however, the innocent man is smart enough to walk away and think, "Too bad buddy, you hurt yourself more than me," then only the guilty person has to come back to learn not to injure others. Don't attempt to do God's work. Be content to do your own and you'll have your hands full.

If you drove down a street and hit a pothole, would you waste your time getting upset about the pothole? Of course not. You wouldn't try to get revenge against the City of Winnipeg. You'd simply remember to avoid that pothole in the future.

This should be your thought process whenever someone wrongs you. Think of it as a learning experience. You have learned a certain person is dangerous. Don't add to your loss by feeling sorry for yourself, hating that person or plotting revenge. Let karma do that. Keep smiling, go on with your life, but be careful when dealing with that person in the future. A bad example can be useful if it teaches us what not to do.

* * *

Hatred is the baby brother of revenge. Hatred doesn't accomplish much except waste your time, waste your energy and give you stomach and liver problems. It makes no sense to hate.

I can forgive someone who has harmed me because I know he'll get what's coming to him sooner or later. But I can't forget. I must keep my guard up so he doesn't hurt me again. Only a fool would put his left hand in the lion's mouth after having his right hand bitten off. Some people interpret this as holding a grudge, but it's really just keeping my distance from the lion. I don't hate the lion, but for my own safety I prefer to play with other, more friendly animals.

* * *

Resentment is an attempt to justify our own failure by explaining it in terms of unfair treatment. There is a certain philosophical victory that comes with resentment. The victim of injustice is morally superior to those who cause the injustice.

Unfortunately, enjoying the victory requires that you remain unhappy so others remember the injustice and continue to realize your superior worth. After a while, this feeling of unhappiness becomes a habit, and you only feel good when you are miserable. If I've got to be miserable to feel good, I'll give up resentment and look for another way to be happy.

* * *

Fear is our choice of reaction to a crisis. Any normal person who is intelligent enough to understand the situation becomes nervous or excited just before a crisis. This life-or-death feeling is probably carried over in our unconscious mind from the days of the cavemen when failure usually meant getting killed. The nervous energy we feel is the additional strength our body supplies us with to help us accomplish our goal.

There are two ways we can use this energy: to fight or flee. If we concentrate on our goal, imagine winning the battle or think, "No matter what happens, I can handle it," the nervous energy turns to courage. But if we forget about our goal and think about all the ways we could fail or think, "I hope nothing happens," our conscious mind switches to flee mode, and the nervous energy fills us with fear.

If we choose to turn and run from our troubles, being in flight mode would be quite helpful, giving us extra speed. But if we want to overcome our difficulty, we should keep our goal in mind and remain in fight mode. We may lose, but since we don't have to fight bears anymore we shouldn't die from the episode.

The boxer Jack Dempsey used to get so nervous before a fight he couldn't shave himself or sit still. He chose not to interpret this nervous energy as fear. In other words, he didn't think about running away from the boxing match. Instead, he went forward, concentrated on his goal and used the energy to put extra power into his punches.

* * *

Accept criticism that is fair and well-intentioned. Ignore the rest. This means approximately ninety percent of the criticism you receive should be ignored. If you're anything like your father, you'll be proud to be yourself and do things your way. Unfortunately, being different invites criticism. You'll need a thicker emotional skin than most people.

We are hurt emotionally, not so much by what people say but by our response to what they say. If we fight back or resent the criticism, we use valuable time and energy that could be spent accomplishing goals. If we don't respond but merely ignore the criticism, it can't hurt us.

The proper attitude toward criticism was demonstrated by Samuel Johnson, the man who wrote the first dictionary. When asked by a woman why he had defined "pastern" as the knee of a horse, he replied, "*Ignorance, madam, pure ignorance.*"

You will come up against many kinds of criticism. Some people, being too proud to ask you to explain something, will accuse you of being wrong in the hope of getting an explanation out of you that way. Others will criticize you because they interpret the situation differently. Some people may want to impress you with their brilliance. Still others have formed the habit of mocking people to prove that everybody else has as many faults as they do.

Whatever the reason, criticism usually boils down to ignorance. Our reaction to criticism should be guided by the following concept: You can't get mad at all the ignorance in the world.

* * *

It's easy to say "don't worry," but how can you stop worrying? This problem is similar to somebody telling you not to think of elephants. The more you try not to think of them, the more elephants you'll think of.

The secret is to fill your mind with thoughts and plans about doing something for someone else. For example, you could think about what you're going to get your father for his birthday. This is always a good thing to think about whenever you want to stop worrying. If it ever slips your mind, feel free to phone me up and I'll remind you.

* * *

Crying

Crying is an outpouring of sadness and selfishness. You never see a bride crying at her wedding. She is purely happy. But the mother cries because she has lost part of her function in life.

If laughter is the best medicine, then crying is the worst poison. Like anger and fear, sorrow brings physical changes to our bodies. The digestion is shut down, the blood pressure is raised, the heart speeds up and the skin becomes cold. Maintained over a long period, this emergency status, this indecisive stewing, will create emotionally induced illness. It is better for our health if we stop feeling sorry for ourselves. We should replace those sad thoughts with pleasant memories and plans for accomplishing future goals.

* * *

Suffering is an exercise that builds inner strength. Like any exercise, too much can do more harm than good. However, tolerating a certain amount of pain now and then increases our resistance to the little aches and pains that accompany life. It doesn't seem to matter if our pain is intentional or accidental; both accomplish the goals of preventing us from being overly sensitive to everyday annoyances.

For example, I have run the marathon and got hit in the family jewels with a hockey puck. I believe that, overall, these experiences have saved me a lot of pain in life because now, getting caught in a rainstorm does not seem so bad. If you do something extra difficult once in a while, it will make the rest of your life seem like a picnic.

* * *

Suffering builds character.

— Jessie Jackson

When you're throwing dirt, you're losing ground.

— Adlai Stevenson

Trouble either brings out the best in people or the worst.

— Unknown

A man can fail many times, but he isn't a failure until he begins to blame somebody else.

— John Burroughs

The superior man is satisfied and composed; the mean man is always full of distress.

— Confucius

The measure of a man is what he does with his power.

— Pittacus, 600 BC

If you attend to your own spiritual growth and improvement, other people will thrive better.

— Freeman Tilden

Don't complain. Do something about it or live with it.

— Perry Ludwig

When asked if one should reward injury with kindness, Confucius answered, "With what then would you reward kindness? Reward injury with justice, reward kindness with kindness."

— Confucius

Men are not hanged for stealing horses, but that horses may not be stolen.

— George Halifax

Beware the man who does not return your blow: He neither forgives you nor allows you to forgive yourself.

— G.B. Shaw

No one can make you feel inferior without your consent.

— Eleanor Roosevelt

What does the moon care if a dog is barking at it?

— Czech proverb

No decent man will condemn me, and I don't care what the rest say.

— Unknown

The stupid never forgive nor forget; the naive forgive and forget; the wise forgive but never forget.

— Thomas Szasz

Politics

GOVERNMENT IS MADE UP of a few smooth-talking politicians plus thousands of bureaucrats whose incomes and careers don't depend on efficient action. These bureaucrats spend more time thinking about how they can get reclassified than how they can help people. The government is an inefficient bureaucratic mess.

Every so often, governments ask their citizens to cooperate in efforts for the "public good." They want you to sacrifice in order to help solve economic problems or military conflicts. These requests can seem compelling and social pressure can build on behalf of patriotic efforts. You have a brain. It's just as intelligent as any politician's. Decide for yourself whether you want to participate in these programs.

Should you join the army and fight for Canada in a war? Every situation has to be analyzed separately; however, self-defence and the protection of females are basic natural instincts. Ants will fight to the last ant to protect their queen. Male buffaloes form a circle to protect their young and females. Yes, I believe if the danger is real we should fight, kill and die, if necessary.

Killing in self-defence is philosophically justified because you are in danger of being killed and it is better for the world if a good person survives than if an evil one does.

* * *

World War II

The Second World War was a significant event in the history of mankind.

I believe Hitler started out as a man with good intentions. He didn't smoke, drink, steal, etc. As he put it—his rise to power was like a fairy tale. At the beginning, everything he did was successful. He improved life in Germany, got people jobs, declared war and took over a few countries, all with virtually no difficulties. Here was a man who might put an end to wars, injustice and poverty. Twice, he was selected as Man of the Year by TIME Magazine. I believe he had a guardian angel helping him during this period.

Then, in 1940 he changed. He became one of the worst leaders in history. He allowed his subordinates to kill innocent people such as Jews, Russians, etc. From that time on, the fairy tale was over and a nightmare began for Hitler. It was like his guardian angel decided Hitler wasn't fit to govern the world and stopped helping him. From then on, everything he did failed. When he needed warm weather for his tanks in Russia, he got the coldest winter in Russian history. When he needed cloudy skies in France so the English planes couldn't fly over and bomb his tanks, he got clear skies. When he needed clear skies to airlift supplies to Stalingrad, he got cloudy skies. Nothing worked, and he lost the war.

I believe this shows good things happen to good people, but if after a little success you stop being a good person, your luck may turn rotten. Your guardian angel may throw up her hands and say, "OK, learn from your mistakes."

The following is taken from a letter written by the German Minister of Armaments to Adolf Hitler, dated March 30, 1945.

> *Unlike so many of your co-workers, I have always spoken frankly to you, and I shall continue to do so...*
>
> *I believe in the future of the German people. I believe in a Providence that is just and inexorable, and thus I believe in God. It pained me deeply during the victorious days of 1940 to see how many among our leaders were losing their inner integrity. This was the moment when we should have commended ourselves to Providence by our decency and*

inner modesty. Then Fate would have been on our side. But during those months, we were weighed in the balance and found too light for ultimate victory. We wasted a year of precious time luxuriating in our easily won success when we could have been girding ourselves for battle. This is why we were caught unprepared in the decisive years of 1944 and 1945. If all our new weapons had been ready a year earlier, we would be in a very different position now. As if we were being warned by Providence, from 1940 on, all our military undertakings were dogged by unprecedented ill luck. Never before has an outside element such as the weather played such a decisive and devastating role as in this, the most technological of all wars: the cold in Moscow, the fog in Stalingrad, and the blue sky above the winter offensive in the West in 1944.

— Albert Speer

* * *

A state is better governed which has but few laws, and those laws strictly enforced.

— René Descartes

The problem with a democracy is that the people can vote themselves benefits from the public treasury.

— Alexander Tytler

Under capitalism man exploits man; under socialism the reverse is true.

— Polish Proverb

Never do anything against conscience, even if State demands it.

— Albert Einstein

The only thing necessary for the triumph of evil is for good men to do nothing.

— Edmund Burke

It's easier to get forgiveness than permission.

— Grace Hopper

Only hit when you have to, but then hit with everything you've got.

— Theodore Roosevelt

Freedom

FREEDOM IS THE OPPORTUNITY to live your life the way you want to. Although you have a lot of control over your situation, you disregard this control when you focus on the people who seem to stand in your way. Concentrate on the things you control and use those things to increase your happiness and the happiness of the world.

You'll never be 100 percent free because every choice brings with it certain consequences. Prince Charles may want to become the King of England but he then loses the freedom to walk into a bar in Southern Ireland. The average person is no more than ten to thirty percent free. But by letting others be free and not trying to change the world, you can reach eighty to ninety percent freedom.

We have seen how foolish it is to waste our time trying to make the world what we think it should be. It is just as foolish to try to make people be what we think they should be. There is no need to change, educate or force anyone to do what we want. I don't think you can really be free unless you're willing to let others be free.

We actually give up a lot of control over our lives when we try to control others. We must first understand their motives and prejudices. Then we must do whatever is necessary to get the desired reaction from them. Our own actions become dictated by what we have to do to control the other person.

By losing the urge to control others, we also lose the need to hate or fear anyone. Since no one has to act in a certain way to please us, there is no need to get upset over what others do.

Letting others be free relieves you of the responsibility for the way they act. You'll experience a wondrous sense of weightlessness, an absence of burdens, the feeling of adventure and challenge that comes with letting the world unfold as it will. You'll know that whatever happens isn't your problem because you are no longer responsible to see that others do what they should. Are people polluting the atmosphere? Let them. Just don't do it yourself.

This attitude will mean you sometimes have to carry a bit more than your share of the load, but that's a small price to pay for not having to keep track of how much everyone else does. If it becomes obvious that you're being taken advantage of, you can just walk away and say, "See you around."

This doesn't mean that you can't speak your mind when you have a difference of opinion with someone. I believe you should take a stand when you feel strongly about something if there is reason to believe your opinion will make a difference. You should learn how to say "no" to others and learn how to make it easy for others to say "no" to you when they want to.

There is nothing wrong with stating your views to people who are important to you. If a friend becomes angry because of something you said or did, you can explain your position to him if he wants to listen. But you don't have to convince him of anything. There are always new, and probably more appropriate, friends. You don't need millions of friends; one or two is plenty.

To reiterate, you are not responsible for the actions of others. You are only responsible for the actions of one person: You. Remember this and you will be free.

* * *

Those who deny freedom to others deserve it not for themselves.

— Abraham Lincoln

Everything that is really great and inspiring is created by the individual who can labor in freedom.

— Albert Einstein

Freedom lies in being bold.

— Robert Frost

Communication

SINCE I HAVEN'T TAKEN any writing courses, I probably shouldn't be giving any advice on this subject. But that didn't stop me from giving advice on all the other topics in this book so I won't stop now.

You should write like you talk. I don't care how technical the subject is, you should write about it as if you're talking to the people who will be reading it.

The present tense is the most emphatic. For example, "He is walking into the cave," is more exciting than the past tense, "He walked into the cave."

The active voice is more direct than the passive voice. "The cow jumped over the moon" is much easier to understand than the passive version, "The moon was jumped over by the cow." The nicest things in life are simple.

Concrete words are preferable to abstract ones. The concrete example, "A good steak might have saved John Keats," reads better than the abstract version, "Administration of proper proteins might have saved John Keats."

I think most people use too many commas, just as the city uses too many stop signs. I also find that I lose concentration when reading a lot of dry theory that doesn't have any interesting examples. Another way to improve your writing is to read it over with a view to taking out the unnecessary words. Very cold is the same as cold.

We write with our unconscious mind. We edit with our conscious. For this reason, the best time to write is first thing in the morning, before a shower, coffee or breakfast. Our conscious mind isn't completely awake yet, so the unconscious has the field to itself. If I review my previous day's writing first thing in the morning, I can easily spot where improvements should be made. It's almost as if the little elves in my unconscious mind worked all night and have all the improvements ready for me by morning. Most of this book was written between four o'clock and six o'clock in the morning. Perhaps I used a bad example.

You can turn off the conscious mind by using the artificial deadline trick. When under extreme time pressure, the conscious mind retreats automatically to allow the unconscious to meet the timetable. If you can fool yourself with an early deadline, you'll still leave time for review and revisions.

When I'm involved in a major project, I have a system that helps keep me organized. At the beginning of the project, I start an idea folder. Then, whenever I get an idea that I may want to use in the report, I write it down and put it in the idea folder. It helps to carry a notebook and pencil around at all times; you never know when you're going to get a neat little idea that may never come back to you again.

When I'm ready to write the report, I separate all the little ideas. Next, I group the related ideas together into sections. Finally, I decide the order I want the sections to be in, and then I'm ready to begin writing the report.

There's no rule that says you have to start writing at the beginning and proceed to the end. If you don't feel in the mood to write a certain section, skip to one that seems more interesting at that time.

Swearing has become quite common in our society. It is usually harmless and in frustrating situations it even seems to relieve tension. However, where it becomes a constant habit, it shows a person with no brains trying to get the feeling of courage.

Making speeches is one area where I have never made a mistake yet. Since I am not prejudiced by past experiences in this field, I can give you an objective viewpoint on the subject.

You will notice most of your nervousness disappearing after making only a couple of public speeches if each time you speak you have the confidence of knowing you did all your homework, you prepared a good text and you now have something valid to share. I'll leave the rest of the speechmaking advice to the experts.

* * *

Every style that is not boring is a good one.

— Voltaire

As to language, it is simply required that it convey the meaning.

— Confucius

The chief virtue that language can have is clearness, and nothing detracts from it so much as the use of unfamiliar words.

— Hippocrates

Don't use metropolis when you're getting paid the same fee for city.

— Mark Twain

Health

GOOD HEALTH IS IMPORTANT so we can live a long life, do good deeds and earn lots of brownie points.

Bioresonance therapy began in Germany in 1990. It uses frequencies to assess and eliminate allergies and other causes of illness. Every substance has its own frequency. The bioresonance machine has an electronic filter that can distinguish between natural healthy vibrations and harmful pathological ones.

A bioresonance therapist has allergen samples that can be used to test the more common foods, metals, pollens, etc. They can also test you for any other substances you want to bring in. Bioresonance therapy will probably reduce or eliminate your allergies without the damaging effects of drugs.

This machine neutralizes the pathological vibrations of toxins, metals, microorganisms and antibodies. This is similar to passing a demagnetizer over magnets stuck on the door of your refrigerator—the magnets would be neutralized and fall off.

Bioresonance therapy has been used worldwide since the year 2000. There are no known side effects. It is completely painless and non-invasive. No electricity enters the body from this device.

* * *

WATER WORKS WONDERS

The following article about drinking water is condensed from the magazine PARADE.

Next to air, water is the substance most necessary for our survival. A normal adult is about 60 to 70 percent water. We can go without food for almost two months but without water only a few days. Yet most people have no idea how much water they should drink. In fact, many live in a dehydrated state.

Without water we'd be poisoned to death by our own waste products. When the kidneys remove uric acid and urea, these must be dissolved in water. If there isn't enough water, wastes are not removed as effectively and may build up as kidney stones. Water is also vital as a medium for chemical reactions in digestion and metabolism. It carries nutrients and oxygen to the cells through the blood and helps to cool the body through perspiration. Water also lubricates our joints.

We even need water to breathe. Our lungs must be moist to take in oxygen and excrete carbon dioxide. We lose a pint of liquid each day just by exhaling.

So if you don't drink sufficient water, you can impair every of your physiology. Dr. Howard Flaks, a bariatric (obesity) specialist in Beverly Hills, Calif., says, "By not drinking enough water, many people incur excess body fat, poor muscle tone and size, decreased digestion efficiency and organ function, increased toxicity in the body, joint and muscle soreness and water retention."

Water retention? If you're not drinking enough, your body may retain water to compensate. Paradoxically, fluid detention can sometimes be eliminated by drinking more water, not less.

"Proper water intake is a key to weight loss," says Dr. Donald Robertson, medical director of the Southwest Bariatric Nutrition Centre in Scottsdale. Ariz. If people who are trying to lose weight don't drink enough water, the body can't metabolize the fat properly. Retaining fluid also keeps weight up."

The minimum for a healthy person is eight to ten eight-ounce glasses a day." Says Dr. Flax. "You need more if you exercise or live in a hot climate.

And overweight people should drink an extra glass for every twenty-five pounds they exceed their ideal weight."

At the International Sports Medicine Institute, we have a formula for water intake: one-half ounce per pound of body weight if you're not active (that's ten eight-ounce glasses a day if your weight is 160bpounds), and two-thirds ounce per pound if you're athletic (13 to 14 glasses a day, at the same weight). Your water intake should be spread through-out the day and evening.

You may wonder: If I drink this much, won't I constantly be running to the bathroom? Initially yes. But after a few weeks your bladder tends to adjust and you urinate less frequently but in larger amounts.

And by consuming those eight to ten glasses of water during your day, you could be well on your way to a healthier leaner body.

— Leroy R. Perry Jr.

* * *

I am not a great believer in material possessions; however, you should never skimp on the following three items:

Mattress—You spend one-third of your life on your mattress. It should be extra firm. Don't ruin your posture by using an old, worn-out mattress.

Shoes—You spend two-thirds of your life in your shoes. It is more important that they be comfortable than stylish. Throw them away if they begin to cause pronation. It's a lot easier to replace your shoes than your knee and hip joints.

Rocking chair—Have one. Rocking soothes the nerves after a hectic day among the noise and haste. Behold the baby, it stops crying when it starts rocking.

* * *

The following are some health tips that I have picked up over the years:

- Eat three almonds a day to prevent tumours.
- Squeeze vitamin E capsules on any burn, including a sunburn.
- Blow, don't sniff.

- Don't worry about having too much cholesterol in your body. Everybody I know who has lived to be over eighty-five years old has eaten lots of eggs, butter and pork fat.
- Exercise 150 minutes a week. This includes walking. It keeps the arteries open.

* * *

Future medicine will be the medicine of frequencies.

— Albert Einstein

Laughter is the best medicine

— Reader's Digest

Quitting smoking is easy. I've done it hundreds of times.

— Mark Twain

Water Works Wonders

NEXT to air, water is the substance most necessary for our survival. A normal adult is about 60- to 70-percent water. We can go without food for almost two months, but without water only a few days. Yet most people have no idea how much water they should drink. In fact, many live in a dehydrated state.

Without water we'd be poisoned to death by our own waste products. When the kidneys remove uric acid and urea, these must be dissolved in water. If there isn't enough water, wastes are not removed as effectively and may build up as kidney stones. Water is also vital as a medium for chemical reactions in digestion and metabolism. It carries nutrients and oxygen to the cells through the blood and helps to cool the body through perspiration. Water also lubricates our joints.

We even need water to breathe: Our lungs must be moist to take in oxygen and excrete carbon dioxide. We lose a pint of liquid each day just exhaling.

So if you don't drink sufficient water, you can impair every aspect of your physiology. Dr. Howard Flaks, a bariatric (obesity) specialist in Beverly Hills, Calif., says, "By not drinking enough water, many people incur excess body fat, poor muscle tone and size, decreased digestive efficiency and organ function, increased toxicity in the body, joint and muscle soreness and water retention."

Water retention? If you're not drinking enough, your body may retain water to compensate. Paradoxically, fluid retention can sometimes be eliminated by drinking *more* water, not less.

"Proper water intake is a key to weight loss," says Dr. Donald Robertson, medical director of the Southwest Bariatric Nutrition Centre in Scottsdale, Ariz. "If people who are trying to lose weight don't drink enough water, the body can't metabolize the fat adequately. Retaining fluid also keeps weight up."

"The minimum for a healthy person is eight to ten eight-ounce glasses a day," says Dr. Flaks. "You need more if you exercise a lot or live in a hot climate. And overweight people should drink an extra glass for every twenty-five pounds they exceed their ideal weight. Consult your own physician for his recommendations."

At the International Sportsmedicine Institute, we have a formula for water intake: one-half ounce per pound of body weight if you're not active (that's ten eight-ounce glasses a day if your weight is 160 pounds), and two-thirds ounce per pound if you're athletic (13 to 14 glasses a day, at the same weight). Your water intake should be spread throughout the day and evening.

You may wonder: If I drink this much, won't I constantly be running to the bathroom? Initially, yes. But after a few weeks your bladder tends to adjust and you urinate less frequently but in larger amounts.

And by consuming those eight to ten glasses of water during your day, you could be well on your way to a healthier, leaner body.

Finances

A FINANCIAL INVESTMENT MEANS gambling with money. The urge to gamble seems to be instinctive in humans. We each have a natural desire to bet on ourselves, take a chance on our creative abilities. When we act boldly, that is exactly what we are doing—gambling on our own talents.

Taking risks is part of life. It's only dangerous when you don't recognize the risks involved. For example, if you let your stockbroker convince you there is no risk in buying a certain stock, you may withdraw your life savings to bet on it. That's dangerous. Never invest more than you can afford to lose.

Few people ever make money on tips. Beware of inside information. If there was any easy money lying around, no one would be stuffing it into your pocket.

at one time or another, most of us have put all our marbles in one basket, timed it just right, and made a tremendous profit. When this happens, the results are usually two-fold. One, it boosts our ego and confidence to the point that we think we can do it at least one more time; second, the profit was made so quickly that we don't consider it in the same light as if it took us several years to earn it.

One of the smartest businessmen I know started out with a horse, a homemade sawmill and a fourth grade education. Over the years, he became a multimillionaire, dealing in land and timber. He made a statement that I have never forgotten. He said, "Boys, when you really make a big profit fast, you have got to get used to having it. Don't do anything with it for six months. By that time, you will be used to having it and you will treat it prudently."

This man had learned something that many of us never learn.

There is one more concept I would like to leave with you. This is not new — it was old when the Phoenicians were trading with the Romans and the Greek Philosophers cornered the olive oil market. The concept is this . . .

The percent gain it takes to recover a loss increases geometrically with the loss. For example, if we lose 15% of our capital, we have to make 17.6% gain on the balance to get even. However, if we lose 30% of our capital, it will take 42.9% gain on the balance we have left to get even; and if we lose 50% of our capital, it will take 100% gain on the balance to get even.

This concept is set out in the little table which follows. I have a copy of this table posted on the wall near my desk as a reminder of the importance of capital management.

% Loss of Initial Capital	% Gain on Balance Required to Recover
5	5.3
10	11.1
15	17.6
20	25.0
25	33.3
30	42.9
35	53.8
40	66.7
45	81.8
50	100.0
55	122.0
60	150.0
65	186.0
70	233.0
75	300.0
80	400.0
85	567.0
90	900.0

Try to stay out of debt. A lot of freedom is lost when you have to spend the present paying off the past.

Never lend a book to anyone unless you don't care if you get it back. If I don't have a backup copy, I don't lend the book. I don't know how many valuable books I've lost by lending them to friends, but I would estimate that about fifty percent of the time you don't get your book back.

A few words about lottery tickets. I think spending a few dollars on them is worth it for the joy of thinking about winning. As an investment, however, you'd probably be better off flushing your money down the toilet and then going for a walk along the river, hoping to find some of it washed up on shore.

* * *

Don't put all your eggs in one basket.

— Miguel Cervantes

There is a tide in the affairs of men, which taken at the flood leads on to fortune.

— Shakespeare

Neither a borrower nor a lender be; for lending oft loses both itself and friend, and borrowing dulls the edge of husbandry.

— Shakespeare

Money gives a man thirty more years of dignity.

— Chinese Proverb

I'd like to live like a poor man with lots of money.

— Pablo Picasso

There are two times in a man's life when he should not speculate: When he can't afford it and when he can.

— Mark Twain

Old Age

IT'S BEEN SAID THAT after the age of forty, a person only thinks of the predominant thoughts of their youth. No matter what our age, we should act young and feel young. Rise each day with a smile on your lips and a song in your heart. Meet the world with a cheerful greeting.

A person of advancing years should not consider himself useless and just wait for death to come for him. He should devote his time to cultivating new talents, studying topics he didn't have time for because of the responsibilities of family and job. All talents are self-earned and are carried over from life to life in our soul. Whatever time, energy and thought we put into acquiring a talent in this life, will contribute to making our next life more creative and interesting.

Realizing that all talents are self-developed should eliminate the emotion of envy in our lives. Whatever talent someone else has, he has earned.

As long as a person has goals to strive for and feels needed by someone or useful to society, they will have what is called "mental energy." This is different from the caloric energy we receive from food. It is something like the electrical energy that makes a motor run. Optimistic, cheerful people who have some reason to be well, increase their mental energy.

When this energy is at an optimum, all our organs function better and we feel good. People with adequate mental energy are better able to fight off disease, heal their wounds and keep looking young. They are known as quick healers. Tests have shown that a pessimistic attitude increases the average length of hospitalization by forty percent.

The length of our lives depends on more than just our mental energy, which is a function of our attitude. What we eat also affects our health. Exercise is another important factor in determining lifespan.

* * *

As a well-spent day brings happy sleep, so life well used brings happy death.

— Leonardo da Vinci

At fifty, everyone has the face they deserve.

— George Orwell

Cowards die many times before their death; the valiant only taste of death but once.

— Shakespeare

I die adoring God, loving my friends, not hating my enemies, and detesting superstition.

— Voltaire

When someone dies over the age of eighty, it is a victory, a cause for celebration, not sadness.

— Stanley Knowles

If I knew I was going to die tomorrow, I would plant a tree today.

— Fred Eggers

I will never be an old man. To me, old age is always fifteen years older than I am.

— Bernard Baruch

Morals

MORALS ARE RULES TO guide your conduct toward what you want and away from what you don't want. The purpose of morals is to prevent you from making a rash decision that could ruin your future.

Clear-cut morals are like a boundary line. If you stay within the boundaries, you'll be able to enjoy yourself freely and spontaneously. You'll be confident that your actions won't cause any problems. If you go beyond your moral boundaries, you can get in trouble.

Choose your morals carefully, and they will serve you well in crisis situations. The worst time to consider long range principles is during an emergency. When our emotions are intense, the unconscious mind takes over. If our free will has not laid out any ground rules, the unconscious will either panic or pick a course of action at random. Either scenario could get you into trouble.

At such times, your principles should be clearly understood. Your only concern should be the specific facts of the situation and how to apply your principles to those facts.

When developing your morals, imagine the various circumstances you may find yourself in. Ask yourself what the consequences of your actions might be. Then decide where to draw the line. Which circumstances deserve a certain response? What change in circumstances would make a different response more appropriate? The result will be your moral rule for that issue.

When you decide on your principles, the rules should be formed in a way that eliminates any need to break them. Recognize exceptions and incorporate them into the rules.

Some rules don't require exceptions. An example would be: "Never form a business partnership." Most of the rules I live by have been mentioned in this book.

It's helpful to write down your rules. You'd be surprised how much more precise you can make a rule once you've seen it on paper. Here are some examples of moral questions that I think should be answered:

1. In what circumstance would you steal, if ever?
2. In what circumstance would you lie, if ever?
3. When would you use physical force to protect yourself? To what extent would you use it to repel an intruder from your property?
4. In what circumstances would you kill, if ever?
5. Would you interfere to stop a fight between a friend and someone else? Between two strangers?
6. In what circumstances would you go to the aid of a stranger?

I would suggest you make a note of everything in this book you think is significant to your life. Hopefully, some things will be. It doesn't matter if you agree with me or not. The important thing is to realize which issues need more study. There are probably many questions which are important to you that I haven't mentioned. As you think of them, make a note of each one so you can consider them more carefully later.

The process of forming a personal morality isn't something that's completed in an hour or two. As your knowledge increases, you'll want to change your rules accordingly. Don't rush. The job may take years, but it's worth it. What could be more stimulating than developing morals that allow you to react creatively and confidently in any crisis?

Humour

THE FOLLOWING IS SOME of my favourite humour:

I asked a Burmese man why women, after centuries of following their men, now walk ahead. He said there were many unexploded land mines since the war.

— Robert Mueller

Abraham Lincoln wrote the Gettysburg Address while travelling from Washington to Gettysburg on the back of an envelope.

— Louis Untermeyer

A youngster, being scolded for a poor report card, asked, "What do you think the trouble with me is, Dad—heredity or environment?"

— Unknown

A young lad is still trying to decipher the following letter from his girlfriend:

Dear Justin,
I hope you are not still angry. I wanted to explain that I was really joking when I told you I didn't mean what I said about reconsidering my decision not to change my mind. Please believe I really mean this.

Love, Karen

If your parents didn't have any children, there's a good chance you won't have any.

— Clarence Day

Do you know when beer tastes the best? When it's in your mouth.

— Unknown

If I'd have known I was going to live this long, I'd have taken better care of my health.

— George Burns on his 82nd birthday

Anyone who goes to see a psychiatrist ought to have his head examined.

— Samuel Goldwyn

Exercise is nonsense. Healthy people don't need it and sick people shouldn't do it.

— Henry Ford

You can observe a lot of things by just watching.

— Yogi Berra

First you forget names, then you forget faces, then you forget to pull your zipper up, then you forget to pull your zipper down.

— Les Rosenberg

A New York cinema has discovered an effective way of getting women to remove their hats. Just before the performance, this notice appears on the screen:
"The management wishes to spare elderly ladies any inconvenience. They are therefore invited to retain their hats."
All hats come off.

— Unknown

An optimistic fellow was wildly enthusiastic about his driving ability. During one trip, his wife consulted a map and informed him they were lost. "We may be lost," he announced, "but we're making good time!"

— Unknown

Two hikers came to the top of a hill and were met by a huge grizzly bear. One of the hikers quickly took off his hiking boots, reached into his knapsack and started putting on his running shoes.
His friend asked, "What are you doing that for? You can't outrun a bear."
"Don't have to," the other replied. "I just have to outrun you."

— Unknown

A Mexican boy was crossing the border into the United States with his bicycle carrier filled with straw. The border guard was convinced the kid was smuggling something, so he carefully examined the straw. Still, he found nothing. Each day the performance was repeated, and each day the guard found nothing, no matter how hard he searched.
After a month of this, the guard said to the boy, "Look, I'm about to be transferred so you can tell me the truth. I give you my word I won't tell, but I'm curious—what are you smuggling?"
"I'm smuggling bicycles," the boy confessed.

— Unknown

* * *

Mark Twain was good for a few laughs. Here are some of his quips:

There ain't no way to find out why a snorer can't hear himself snore.

Reports of my death are greatly exaggerated. (Cable to The Associated Press on learning that his obituary had been published.)

Scarce, sir. Mighty scarce. (Responding to the question—In a world without women, what would men become?)

* * *

Winston Churchill had a unique thought process. Here is some of my favourite Churchillian humour:

A woman on a train once said to Churchill, "Sir, you're drunk." Churchill replied, "Madame, you're ugly, and I'll be sober in the morning."

A new member of parliament went up to Churchill and said, "Sir, this is my first day in Parliament. I guess I should make a speech or everyone will wonder why I don't speak."

Churchill replied, "Better they wonder why you don't speak than wonder why you do."

An admirer of Winston Churchill gushed, "Doesn't it thrill you to know that every time you make a speech the auditorium is filled to overflowing?"

"It's flattering," he admitted, "but then I always realize that if instead of making a speech, I was being hanged, the crowd would be three times as big!"

At his London home in Hyde Park Gate, Sir Winston Churchill celebrated his eighty-second birthday. After posing for photographers, a cameraman called out:

"Sir Winston! I hope to take your picture on your hundredth birthday."

Sir Winston turned and regarded the well-wisher with a scorching glare leavened with a trace of a smile. "I see no reason why you shouldn't, young man," he rumbled. "You look hale and hearty enough."

Lady Nancy Astor, who was noted for her sharp tongue, once got annoyed with Churchill.

"Winston," she said sharply, "if you were my husband I'd put poison in your coffee."

"Nancy," replied Churchill, "if I were your husband I'd drink that coffee."

* * *

Those who know laughter have learned the secret of living. They have discovered that life is a wonderful game.

— George Sheehan

Puzzles

HERE ARE SOME OF my favourite puzzles:

1. The Monkey Puzzle: A rope is passed over a frictionless pulley. It has a ten-pound weight at one end, and a ten-pound monkey at the other. There is the same length of rope on either side. If the monkey climbs up the rope, will the weight go up, down or stay in the same place?

   — Lewis Carroll

2. The Squirrel Puzzle: A squirrel in a one meter long log takes ten seconds to run from one end of the log to the other. If the squirrel then starts running back and forth, doubling his speed each time, how long will it take for him to stick his head out of both ends of the log at once?

   — Unknown

3. The Canary Puzzle: A truck carrying a load of canaries is weighed while the canaries are sitting on the floor of the truck. Then the driver hits the truck box with a stick and all the birds start flying. Will the weight go up, down or remain the same?

   — Unknown

4. The Four Triangles Puzzle: You are given six matches and asked to form the outline of four equilateral triangles with them. How do you do it?

— Presh Talwalkar

5. The Rabbit and Turtle Puzzle: The rabbit and the turtle decide to have a race. Since the rabbit runs twice as fast as the turtle, the turtle was given a 100-metre lead. When the race started, the rabbit ran to where the turtle started, but by then the turtle was fifty meters ahead. This continued many times. Whenever the rabbit caught up to where the turtle had been, the turtle was half the distance ahead. Eventually, the distance between them was very small, but the rabbit could never catch the turtle. True or false?

— Unknown

6. Proof that 2 = 1

Let	a = b
X a	a2 = ab
- b2	a2 - b2 = ab - b2
Factor	(a - b) (a + b) = b (a - b)
Cancel	a + b = b
Add	2b = b
/ b	2 = 1

— John Hush

7. The False Coin Puzzle: You have twelve coins and a balance scale. The coins may be all the same weight, or one coin may be lighter or heavier than the rest. Show how, in three weighing's, you can determine if they are identical, or which coin is different and whether it is lighter or heavier.

— Chris Higgens

8. ABLE WAS I ERE I SAW ELBA

— Napoleon

9. The Zebra puzzle below is an excellent puzzle when you have lots of time and nothing to do, such as if you are in jail or work for the government.

The Zebra Puzzle: Calculate who owns the zebra given the following facts:

1. There are five houses, each of a different colour and inhabited by men of different nationalities with different pets, drinks and cigarettes.

2. The Englishman lives in the red house.

3. The Spaniard owns one dog.

4. Coffee is drunk in the green house.

5. The Ukrainian drinks tea.

6. The green house is immediately to the right (your right) of the ivory house.

7. The Old Gold smoker owns snails.

8. Kools are smoked in the yellow house.

9. Milk is drunk in the middle house.

10. The Norwegian lives in the first house of the left.

11. The man who smokes Chesterfields lives in the house next to the man with the fox.

12. Kools are smoked in the house next to the house where the horse is kept.

13. The Lucky Strikes smoker drinks orange juice.

14. The Japanese smokes Parliaments.

15. The Norwegian lives next to the blue house.

— Albert Einstein

Conclusion

SO THAT'S ABOUT ALL I know, my son. My ideas are based on my experiences. Your experiences will be different, so your ideas will be different. This is normal and good. I hope my theories give you food for thought while you are developing your own philosophy of life.

Initially, I intended to give you a "manual of life" written by someone else. Many people have produced such a guide, including Bertrand Russell, Francis Bacon and Ralph Waldo Emerson. Unfortunately, I do not agree with their basic philosophies. Maxwell Maltz has most of the answers. Edgar Cayce has them all, but he speaks in a biblical dialect. I finally decided to write my own version of the truth, combining Maltz psychology with Cayce philosophy. Hope you like it.

So, in your life, have a lot of laughs and try to sneak in a few good deeds now and then. Thanks for being a respectful son. You have been a real source of pride to your mother and I. And I'd like you to know I really enjoy being your father.

Love forever,

Dad

Afterword

THE WORST PART ABOUT marriages that end in divorce is the unintended consequences it has on the children. This book was written for my son with the goal to make up for the fact that I wasn't with him every day to help him navigate life's challenges. My son is a grown man now with a career and a family of his own. He is about the same age as I was when I wrote the book for him thirty years ago. It's incredible how fast the years fly by. I'm happy to report that my son's life turned out fine, although I cannot prove it is because of my book. Advice in written form is a poor replacement for spending actual time together, building memories and sharing stories. We did that whenever the visitation schedule allowed, but it was not nearly enough for me. I would have preferred to have listened to him more, encouraged him more and laughed with him more. But instead of looking back with regret, I choose to celebrate the gift that is my life. I am not always perfect but I lived the best life I could, based on the principles and philosophy reflected in this book. I tried to be a good person and make the world a better place. I end with the sincere hope that you too will live your best life and contribute to the world in a meaningful and positive way.

Thank you for reading this book.

— DML

Definitions

THE FOLLOWING DEFINITIONS ARE quotes from wise people.

The beginning of wisdom is the definition of terms.

— Socrates

Conscious mind—that part of our brain which we use to decide our morals and goals in life. Also known as free will or forebrain, the conscious mind is located in the left side of the brain. It can access information and creative ideas from the unconscious mind.

— Maxwell Maltz

Emotion—an involuntary reaction that occurs as a result of our previous experiences.

— Harry Browne

Envy—the desire for something possessed by someone else.

— Maxwell Maltz

Freedom—the opportunity to live your life as you want to live it.

— Harry Browne

Free will—the force in our conscious mind which is developing either with or against nature.

— Maxwell Maltz

Guilt—the unlived life.

— George Sheehan

Happiness—the mental feeling of well-being.

— Harry Browne

Immoral—hurting someone selfishly.

— Dennis Ludwig

Integrity—knowing yourself well enough to be able to mean what you say.

— Harry Browne

Intuition—the unconscious use of information learned from previous experiences.

— Harry Browne

Jealousy—the negative emotion caused by the fear of losing someone (or something) to someone else.

— Harry Browne

Justice—the natural, inevitable consequence that follows every act.

— Harry Browne

Karma—the abacus on which gains and losses of the soul are scored from life to life.

— Edgar Cayce

Knowledge—holding onto what you know and admitting what you don't know.

— Confucius

Life—habitation of a body by a soul, for a limited period of time.

— Edgar Cayce

Love—the emotion of wanting to give to, and grow with, another person.

— Edgar Cayce

Mental energy—the name given to the energy which flows through our body. This energy increases with optimistic, cheerful thought.

Also known as adaptation energy (Selye), elan vital (Bergson), vital energy (Cayce) or life force (Maltz).

Morals—rules to guide your conduct toward what you want and away from what you don't want.

— Harry Browne

Natural monopoly—a situation in which you are so appropriate to the needs and desires of your customers, friends or lover, that competition is relatively powerless to affect the relationship.

— Harry Browne

Non-marriage—a love relationship in which no attempt is made to merge property, uncommon interests or decision-making authority.

— Harry Browne

Partnership—an agreement in which responsibilities and rewards will be shared.

— Harry Browne

Patriotism—your conviction that this country is superior to all other countries because you were born in it.

— G.B. Shaw

Person—a soul inhabiting a body.

— Edgar Cayce

Reincarnation—a belief that the soul is eternal, and at intervals appears again in other physical bodies, so that it can continue its own development.

— Edgar Cayce

Religion—the service and worship of God or the supernatural.

— Merriam-Webster Dictionary

Selfishness—concern with your own happiness when it is harmful to society.

— Harry Browne

Sin—the failure to reach your potential.

— George Sheehan

Soul—an electromagnetic force containing everything we have learned and experienced in past lives. Also known as psyche or spirit.

— Edgar Cayce

Success—the knowledge that you have become yourself, the person you were meant to be from all time.

— George Sheehan

Truth—information that leads to predictable results.

— Unknown

Unconscious mind—that part of our brain which contains all our experiences and knowledge gained in this life. The unconscious mind can also tune in to information stored in our soul, much like a TV set can pick up electrical signals. It is located in the right side of our brain, the hemisphere of intuition and creativity.

— Maltz and Cayce

Unhappiness—the mental feeling of discomfort.

— Harry Browne

Work—anything a person has to do.

— Mark Twain

Play—anything a person doesn't have to do.

— Mark Twain

References

Bartlett, John. *Familiar Quotations.* Little Brown & Company, 1968.

Only 1,540 pages long. A good book to memorize.

Browne, Harry, *How I Found Freedom in an Unfree World.* Liam Works, 1973.

The author, a financial investment advisor, explains his philosophy of life. He has some ingenious ideas on how to handle life's troublesome situations.

Cernimara, Gina. *Many Mansions: The Edgar Cayce Story on Reincarnation.* Morrow edition, 1968.

This book is about reincarnation as viewed by Edgar Cayce. It is the basis for the philosophical sections of your manual.

Maltz, Maxwell. *Psycho-Cybernetics.* Simon & Schuster, 1960.

This is a psychology book written by a plastic surgeon. A majority of my ideas come from this book.

CPSIA information can be obtained
at www.ICGtesting.com
Printed in the USA
BVHW022327090622
639360BV00002B/8

9 781039 134379